Irish Crochet Designs and Projects

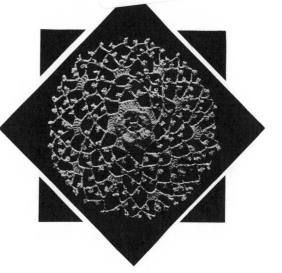

Edited by Mary Carolyn Waldrep

DOVER PUBLICATIONS, INC.

New York

CROCHET ABBREVIATIONS

bal	balance	rnd	round
bl OR blk	block	rpt	repeat
ch	chain	sc	single crochet
dc	double crochet	s dc	short double crochet
dec	decrease	sk	skip
d tr	double treble	sl st	slip stitch
h dc	half double crochet	sp	space
inc	increase	st(s)	stitch(es)
incl	inclusive	tog	together
lp	loop	tr OR trc	treble crochet
p	picot	tr tr	triple treble (yarn
pc st	popcorn stitch		over hook 4 times)

* (asterisk) or † (dagger) . . . Repeat the instructions following the asterisk or dagger as many times as specified.

** or †† . . . Used for a second set of repeats within one set of instructions.

Repeat instructions in parentheses as many times as specified. For example: "**(Ch 5, sc in next sc) 5 times**" means to work all that is in parentheses 5 times.

Copyright © 1988 by Dover Publications, Inc.
All rights reserved under Pan American and International
Copyright Conventions.

Published in Canada by General Publishing Company, Ltd.,
30 Lesmill Road, Don Mills, Toronto, Ontario.
Published in the United Kingdom by Constable and Company,
Ltd.

This Dover edition, first published in 1988, is a new selection of patterns from *Centerpieces, Book No. 276,* published by The Spool Cotton Company, New York, 1951; *Doilies, Book No. 201,* published by The Spool Cotton Company, 1943; *Matching Sets in Crochet, Book No. 281,* published by The Clark Thread Company, Inc., New York, 1951; *Bedspreads to Knit and Crochet, Book No. 186,* published by The Spool Cotton Company, 1942; *Revised Beginner's Manual, Star Book No. 62, 3rd Edition,* published by the American Thread Company, New York, 1948; *Edgings: Crocheted, Tatted, Hair Pin Lace, Star Book No. 81,* published by the American Thread Company, 1951; *Laces and Edgings, Book No. 199,* published by The Spool Cotton Company, 1943; *Hand Crochet by Royal Society: Laces and Doilies, Book No. 3,* published by Royal Society, Inc., New York, 1943; *Doilies to Treasure, Book 1600,* published by Lily Mills Company, Shelby, North Carolina, n.d.; *A Complete Collection of Crochet Designs: Edgings, Insertions, Doilies, Medallions, Antimacassars, Bedspreads,* published by The Spool Cotton Company, 1932; *Crocheted Bedspreads & Novelties, Book No. 6-B,* published by Lily Mills Company, 1937; *Clark's O. N. T. Crocheted Collars, Book 68,* published by The Spool Cotton Company, 1936; *Correct Table Settings, Book No. 260,* published by The Spool Cotton Company, 1949; *Star Book of Doilies, Book 22,* published by the American Thread Company, n.d.; *Doilies, Book No. 12,* published by Royal Society, Inc., 1951; *Place Mats and Doilies, Book No. 315,* published by Coats & Clark Inc., New York, 1955; *Bedspreads, Book No. 151,* published by The Spool Cotton Company, 1940; *Edgings: 100 Old and New Favorites!, Book No. 218,* published by The Spool Cotton Company, 1945; *Doilies—in the Modern Manner, Book No. 297,* published by Coats & Clark Inc., 1953; *Treasure Chest of Crochet, Star Book No. 45,* published by the American Thread Company, 1946; *Motifs in Crochet, Design Book No. 68,* published by Lily Mills Company, 1953; *Dorothea Creations: Crocheted Luncheon Sets, Dinner Cloths, Bedspreads and Matching Articles, Vol. 21,* published by Alfred Mayer-Weismann & Co., Boston, Massachusetts, 1941; Coats & Clark's *Hostess Book, Book No. 325,* published by Coats & Clark Inc., 1956; *Doilies, Doilies and More Doilies, Star Doily Book No. 120,* published by the American Thread Company, 1955; *Hand Crochet by Royal Society for Babies, Book No. 2,* published by Royal Society, Inc., 1943.

Manufactured in the United States of America
Dover Publications, Inc.
31 East 2nd Street
Mineola, N.Y. 11501

Library of Congress Cataloging-in-Publication Data

Irish crochet designs and projects.

1. Irish crochet lace. 2. Crocheting—Ireland. I. Waldrep, Mary Carolyn.
TT805.I74 1988   746.2′2   88-3707
ISBN 0-486-25690-1

Introduction

The intricate, richly ornamented form of needlework known as Irish crochet was originally developed in the mid-nineteenth century as a means of imitating expensive Venetian point laces. In its original form, individual motifs—leaves, flowers, buds, tendrils, rings, etc.—were crocheted separately and tacked to a fabric foundation. The background was then filled in with a crocheted mesh. Patterns rarely gave instructions for joining the motifs; the worker was told to "follow her own artistic instinct" and left to work out the details for herself.

Fortunately for the modern needleworker, by the 1920s and 30s, patterns for Irish crochet had become more detailed, and row-by-row instructions for beautiful bedspreads, doilies, tablecloths, edgings and other items were widely available. In this volume, we offer some of the finest Irish crochet designs from now rare thread company leaflets of the 1930s, 40s and 50s. Modern technology allows us to present them to you just as they originally appeared. Many of the threads listed in the instructions are still available; if not, similar threads that will give the same gauge can easily be found. Be very careful when purchasing threads, however, because some product names used in the past are now being reused on entirely different products. Such is the case with the Lustersheen mentioned on page 27.

For best results, you should have the same number of stitches and rows as indicated in the instructions. Before beginning a project, make a small sample of the pattern, working with the suggested hook size and desired thread. If your work is too tight, use a larger hook; if it is too loose, use a smaller hook.

To give your project a professional look, you should wash and block it. For large projects that are made up of many units sewn together, you may find it easier to block the individual pieces before joining them. Use a neutral soap and cool water. Gently squeeze the suds through the crochet; do not rub. Rinse thoroughly. If desired, starch the piece lightly. Pad a flat surface with several layers of thick terry toweling. Using rustproof pins, pin the piece, right side down, on the surface, pinning each picot and loop in place. If the work has three-dimensional flowers, pin it to the surface with the right side *up*, rather than down. When the crochet is almost dry, press it through a damp cloth with a moderately hot iron. Do not allow the iron to rest on the stitches, particularly the raised stitches.

The terminology and hooks listed in this book are those used in the United States. The following charts give the U.S. names of crochet stitches and their equivalents in other countries and the approximate equivalents to U.S. crochet hook sizes. Crocheters should become thoroughly familiar with the differences in both crochet terms and hook sizes before starting any project.

The stitches used in the projects in this book are explained on page 47. A metric conversion chart is located on page 48.

STITCH CONVERSION CHART

U.S. Name	Equivalent
Chain	Chain
Slip	Single crochet
Single crochet	Double crochet
Half-double or short-double crochet	Half-treble crochet
Double crochet	Treble crochet
Treble crochet	Double-treble crochet
Double-treble crochet	Treble-treble crochet
Treble-treble or long-treble crochet	Quadruple-treble crochet
Afghan stitch	Tricot crochet

STEEL CROCHET HOOK CONVERSION CHART

U.S. Size	00	0	1	2	3	4	5	6	7	8	9	10	11	12	13	14
British & Canadian Size	000	00	0	1	–	1½	2	2½	–	3	–	4	–	5	–	6
Metric Size (mm)	3.00	2.75	2.50	2.25	2.10	2.00	1.90	1.80	1.65	1.50	1.40	1.25	1.10	1.00	0.75	0.60

Peacock Tails

MATERIALS:

J. & P. Coats Best Six Cord Mercerized Crochet, Art. A.104, Size 30: 6 Balls of White . . . Milwards Steel Crochet Hook No. 10 . . . A piece of pink linen, 27 inches in diameter.

Centerpiece measures 35 inches in diameter.

GAUGE: Triangular motif measures 3½ x 4½ inches. Round motif measures 4¼ inches in diameter.

FIRST TRIANGULAR MOTIF . . .
Starting at center, ch 20. **1st row:** Sc in 2nd ch from hook and in each ch across, ch 9; working along opposite side of starting chain make sc in each of 19 ch across, ch 4, sc in each of the 19 sc first made. Ch 7, turn. **2nd row:** Picking up back loop only of each sc throughout, make sc in each of the next 19 sc, in ch-4 loop make 2 sc, ch 4 and 2 sc; sc in next 19 sc. Ch 7, turn. **3rd row:** Sc in next 21 sc, in ch-4 sp make 2 sc, ch 4 and 2 sc; sc in each remaining sc across to within last 2 sc. Ch 7, turn. **4th to 9th rows incl:** Sc in each sc to ch-4 sp, in ch-4 sp make 2 sc, ch 4 and 2 sc; sc in each remaining sc across to within last 2 sc. Ch 7, turn.
Now work Edging in rnds as follows: **1st rnd:** Ch 5, sc in next ch-7 loop, (ch 4, sc in next loop) 8 times; (ch 5, skip next 4 sc, picking up both loops make sc in next sc) 5 times; (ch 5, sc in ch-4 loop) twice; (ch 5, skip 4 sc, sc in next sc) 5 times. **2nd rnd:** (Ch 2, in next loop make dc, ch 3 and dc) 16 times; ch 3, dc in same loop as last dc (tip), (ch 2, in next loop make dc, ch 3 and dc) 5 times. **3rd rnd:** * Ch 2, in next ch-3 sp make 2 dc, ch 3 and 2 dc (shell made). Repeat from * around (22 shells on rnd). **4th rnd:** * Ch 3, shell in ch-3 sp of next shell. Repeat from * around (22 shells). **5th rnd:** * Ch 3, sc in next ch-3 sp, ch 3, in ch-3 sp of next shell make (sc, ch 5) 3 times and sc (picot-group made). Repeat from * around (22 picot-groups), ch 3, join with sl st to first sc made. Break off.

SECOND TRIANGULAR MOTIF
. . . Work as for First Motif until 4 rnds of Edging are completed. **5th rnd:** (Ch 3, sc in next ch-3 sp, ch 3, in ch-3 sp of next shell make sc, ch 5, sc, ch 2, sl st in corresponding ch-5 loop on First Motif, sc in same place as last sc on Second Motif, ch 5, sc in same place as last sc) twice; ch 3, sc in next ch-3 sp and complete rnd as for First Motif, joining the last 2 picot groups to adjacent picot groups of First Motif as before. Join and break off.

Make 21 more motifs, joining them to previous motif as Second Motif was joined to First Motif and joining last motif to previous motif and to First Motif made.

FIRST ROUND MOTIF—Center Wheel . . .
Wind thread around first finger of left hand 25 times, slip off. **1st rnd:** Make 48 sc in ring. Join with sl st. **2nd rnd:** Sc in same place as sl st, * ch 4, skip 2 sc, dc in next sc, (ch 5, sc in top of dc) 3 times (a triple picot made); ch 3, skip 2 sc, sc in next sc. Repeat from * around (8 triple picots). Join and break off.

SECOND WHEEL . . .
Work as for Center Wheel until 1st rnd is completed. **2nd rnd:** Ch 4, skip 2 sc, dc in next sc, ch 5, sc in top of dc, ch 2, sl st in center picot of any triple picot on Center Wheel, ch 3, sc in top of dc on Second Wheel, ch 5, sc in same place as last sc, ch 3, skip 2 sc, sc in next sc, ch 4, skip 2 sc, dc in next sc, make a triple picot, joining it to next triple picot on Center Wheel as before, ch 3, skip 2 sc, sc in next sc, ch 4, skip 2 sc, dc in next sc, make a triple picot (do not join), ch 3, skip 2 sc, sc in next sc, ch 4, dc in next sc, ch 5, sc in top of dc, ch 2, sl st in center ch-5 loop of free picot group preceding joining on outer edge of First and Second Triangular Motifs, ch 2, sc in top of dc on Wheel Motif, ch 5, sc in same place, continue to work in pattern, joining next triple picot to next picot group on same motif, join next 2 triple picots to next 2 picot groups following

joining on Second Triangular Motif, make 1 more triple picot, sl st in first sc. Break off.

THIRD WHEEL . . .
Work as before until 1st rnd is completed. **2nd rnd:** Work in pattern, joining first triple picot to first free triple picot preceding joining on Center Wheel, join next triple picot to next free triple picot on Second Wheel, join next 2 triple picots to next 2 picot groups on Second Triangular Motif and complete rnd in pattern (no more joinings). Break off.

FOURTH WHEEL . . .
Work as before, joining first triple picot to next triple picot on Center Wheel, joining next 2 triple picots to next 2 free triple picots on previous wheel and complete rnd in pattern (no more joinings). Break off.

FIFTH WHEEL . . .
Work as before, joining the next 2 triple picots to next 2 triple picots on Center Wheel and next triple picot to next free triple picot on preceding wheel (no more joinings). Break off.

SIXTH WHEEL . . .
Join to correspond with Fourth Wheel.

SEVENTH WHEEL . . .
Join to correspond with Third Wheel. Break off. This completes one round motif.
Work round motifs in this manner around, joining 5th and 6th triple picots of each Third Wheel to adjacent free picot on Seventh (last) Wheel of previous Round Motif as before. Join last Round Motif to First Round Motif in same way.
Place motifs on linen, trace around inner edge, leaving ⅛ inch for hem. Cut out material in back of motifs and sew motifs and hem neatly in place. Starch lightly and press.

Shannon Star

MATERIALS:

J. & P. COATS or CLARK'S O.N.T. BEST SIX CORD MERCERIZED CROCHET, Size 50:

J. & P. Coats —1 ball of White or Ecru,

or

Clark's O.N.T.—2 balls of White or Ecru.

Steel Crochet Hook No. 12.

Starting at center, ch 9, join with sl st. **1st rnd:** 16 sc in ring, sl st in 1st sc made. **2nd rnd:** Sc in same place as sl st, * ch 5, skip 1 sc, sc in next sc. Repeat from * around, ending with ch 5. **3rd rnd:** * Sc in next sc, 2 sc in ch-5 sp, ch 4. Repeat from * around. **4th to 15th rnds incl:** * Skip 1st sc, sc in each remaining sc of sc group, 2 sc in ch-4 sp, ch 4. Repeat from * around (15 sc in each sc group on last rnd). **16th rnd:** * Skip 1 sc, sc in next 13 sc, ch 4, sc in ch-4 sp, ch 4. Repeat from *. **17th rnd:** * Skip 1 sc, sc in next 11 sc; (ch 5, sc in next loop) twice; ch 5. Repeat from * around. Continue in this manner, having 2 sc less in each sc group and 1 loop more between sc groups on each rnd, until 1 sc remains in each sc group, ending with ch 5, sc in loop preceding 1st sc.

Now work as follows: **1st rnd:** * Ch 2, sc in next loop; (ch 5, sc in next loop) 7 times. Repeat from * around, ending with sc in loop preceding 1st ch-2. **2nd rnd:** * 5 dc in ch-2 loop, sc in next loop, (ch 5, sc in next loop) 6 times. Repeat from * around, ending with ch 5, sc in center st of dc group. **3rd rnd:** * (Ch 5, sc in next loop) 6 times; ch 5, sc in center st of next dc group. Repeat from * around, ending with sc in last loop of previous rnd. **4th rnd:** 5 dc in next sc (directly above previous dc group), sc in next loop, then work ch-5 loops around, working 5 dc in the sc directly above previous dc groups. **5th rnd:** Work ch-6 loops around, working sc in center st of dc group. **6th rnd:** Work ch-6 loops around, making 7 dc in sc directly over dc group below. **7th rnd:** Work ch-7 loops around. **8th rnd:** Work ch-8 loops around, ending with sc in loop before the loop above dc group. **9th rnd:** Ch 8, * in next loop (directly above dc groups) work 4 3-d tr clusters with ch 5 between. Clusters are made as follows: Holding back the last loop of each d tr on hook work 3 d tr in same place, thread over and draw through all loops on hook. Ch 8 after last cluster, then (sc in next loop, ch 8) 6 times. Repeat from * around, ending with sc under the ch-8 just before 1st cluster. Fasten off.

Large Motif (Make 8) . . . Starting at center, ch 15. Join with sl st to form ring. **1st rnd:** Ch 1, work 26 sc in ring. Join with sl st in 1st sc. **2nd rnd:** Ch 4, * dc in next sc, ch 1. Repeat from * around. Join to 3rd st of ch-4 first made (26 sps). **3rd rnd:** 2 sc in each sp around. Join (52 sc). **4th rnd:** Ch 4, then work tr in each sc around, increasing 8 tr in the rnd—*to inc, make 2 tr in 1 st.* Join (60 tr). **5th rnd:** Sc in same place as sl st, * ch 2, skip 2 sts, tr in next st; d tr in each of next 5 sts with ch 2 between; ch 2, tr in next st, ch 2, skip 2 sts, sc in next st. Repeat from * around. Join (5 fans). **6th rnd:** * 2 sc in next sp; in each of next 6 sps make 2 sc, ch 3 and 2 sc; work 2 sc in next sp. Repeat from * around; sl st in 1st sc made. Fasten off.

Rosette (Make 8) . . . Starting at center, ch 10, join with sl st to form ring. **1st rnd:** Ch 1, work 20 sc in ring. Join with sl st in 1st sc. **2nd rnd:** Ch 1, sc in same place as sl st, * ch 5, skip 3 sc, sc in next sc. Repeat from * around. Join last ch-5 with sl st in 1st sc. **3rd rnd:** In each loop around make sc, h dc, 5 dc, h dc and sc. Join. **4th rnd:** * Ch 6, sc between sc's of next 2 petals. Repeat from * around. Join. **5th rnd:** Make a petal in each loop, having 7 dc instead of 5 dc on each petal. **6th rnd:** Work as for 4th rnd, making ch 7 (instead of ch-6). **7th rnd:** Same as 5th rnd, making 9 dc (instead of 7). Fasten off.

Sew motifs and rosettes to doily as in illustration.

Valentine

MATERIALS:

**CLARK'S O.N.T. BEST SIX CORD MER-
CERIZED CROCHET,** Art. B.4, Size
50: 5 balls of White for Centerpiece
and 15 balls for Runner; or

Clark's Big Ball Mercerized Crochet,
Art. B.34, Size 50: 2 balls of White
for Centerpiece and 4 balls for
Runner.

A few yards of White Pearl Cotton.

Milwards Steel Crochet Hook No. 12.

½ yard of aqua linen, 36 inches wide.

Centerpiece measures 14½ inches in
diameter; Runner measures 14½ x
42 inches.

CENTERPIECE—Edging—Rose . . .

Starting at center, ch 7. Join with sl st
to form ring. **1st rnd:** Ch 6, (dc in
ring, ch 3) 6 times. Join with sl st
to 3rd ch of ch-6 (7 sps). **2nd rnd:**
In each sp around make sc, 8 dc and sc.
3rd rnd: * Ch 5, sc (from back of
work) in next dc on first rnd. Repeat
from * around, ending with ch 5, sc
in same place as sl st on first rnd.
4th rnd: In each loop around make sc,
10 dc and sc. **5th rnd:** * Ch 6, sc in
the sc between next 2 petals on 3rd
rnd. Repeat from * around, ending

with sc between last and first petals.
6th rnd: In each loop around make
sc, 12 dc and sc. **7th rnd:** * Ch 7,
sc in the sc between next 2 petals on
5th rnd. Repeat from * around. **8th
rnd:** In each loop around make sc, 14
dc and sc. **9th rnd:** Sl st to 3rd dc
of first petal, sc in same place, * (ch 6,
sl st in 4th ch from hook—picot made
—ch 2, picot, ch 2, skip 3 dc, sc in
next dc) twice; (ch 2, picot) twice;
ch 2, sc in 3rd dc of next petal. Repeat
from * around, ending with sl st in
first sc. **10th and 11th rnds:** Sl st to
center of next loop, sc in same loop,
* (ch 2, picot) twice; ch 2, sc in
next loop. Repeat from * around, ending with sl st in first sc. Break off at
end of 11th rnd.

THISTLE . . . 1st rnd:

Wind thread
20 times around a match, slip off and
make 21 sc in ring. Join with sl st to
first sc. **2nd rnd:** Ch 6, * tr in next sc,
ch 2. Repeat from * around. Join last
ch-2 with sl st to 4th ch of ch-6
(21 sps). **3rd rnd:** Working over 2
strands of Pearl Cotton make 4 sc in
each sp around. Join. Break off the
2 strands. **4th rnd:** Sc in same place
as sl st, * ch 4, sc in front loop of
next sc. Repeat from * around, ending
with sl st in first sc. **5th rnd:** Sc in

same place as sl st, * (ch 2, picot)
twice; ch 2, skip 3 sc, sc in back of
next sc. Repeat from * around. Join
with sl st to first sc. **6th rnd:** Repeat
10th rnd of Rose. **7th rnd:** Sl st to
center of next loop, sc in same loop,
ch 2, picot, ch 1, sl st in any loop on
last rnd of Rose, ch 1, picot, ch 2,
sc in next loop on Thistle and complete
as for last rnd of Rose, joining 2nd
and 3rd loops to corresponding loops
of Rose as first loop was joined.

Make 5 more Roses and 5 more
Thistles, joining them in alternate
order as shown in illustration as first
Thistle was joined to Rose, and having
9 free loops on outer edge and 6 free
loops on inner edge.

Now work around inner edge as
follows: **1st rnd:** Attach thread to 2nd
free loop on any flower, sc in same
place, * (ch 2, picot) twice; ch 2,
sc in next loop. Repeat from * 3 more
times; ch 2, picot, ch 2, sc in next
free loop on next flower, turn, (ch 2,
picot) twice; ch 2, sc in last loop on
previous flower, turn, (ch 2, picot)
twice; ch 2, sc in last loop made, ch 2,
picot, ch 2, sc in next free loop on
flower, (ch 2, picot) twice; ch 2 and
continue thus around. Join and break
off. Lay this piece aside.

(Continued on page 9)

7

Talisman

MATERIALS:
CLARK'S O.N.T. or J. & P. COATS
BEST SIX CORD MERCERIZED CROCHET, size 20:

SINGLE SIZE	DOUBLE SIZE
SMALL BALL:	SMALL BALL:
CLARK'S O.N.T.—210 balls,	CLARK'S O.N.T.—257 balls,
OR	OR
J. & P. COATS —120 balls.	J. & P. COATS —147 balls.
BIG BALL:	BIG BALL:
J. & P. COATS —70 balls.	J. & P. COATS —86 balls.

Steel crochet hook No. 8 or 9.

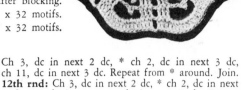

GAUGE: Each motif measures 3¼ inches in diameter after blocking. For a single size spread about 72 x 105 inches, make 22 x 32 motifs. For a double size spread about 88 x 105 inches, make 27 x 32 motifs.

MOTIF . . . Starting at center, ch 10. Join. **1st rnd:** Ch 1, 18 sc in ring. Sl st in 1st sc made. **2nd rnd:** * Ch 5, skip 2 sc, sc in next sc. Repeat from * 5 times; ch 5. **3rd rnd:** In each loop around make sc, h dc, 5 dc, h dc and sc (6 petals). **4th rnd:** Ch 7, insert hook in next loop from back to front of work, bring it out in next loop from front to back of work; thread over, draw loop through, thread over and draw through all loops on hook. Make 4 more ch-7 loops, then ch 7. **5th rnd:** In each loop around make sc, h dc, dc, 7 tr, dc, h dc and sc (6 petals). **6th rnd:** Same as 4th rnd, only joining last ch-7 with sl st in 1st loop (6 loops).

7th rnd: Ch 3, 7 dc in same loop, 8 dc in each loop around (48 dc in rnd), sl st in 3rd st of ch-3 first made. **8th rnd:** Ch 3, dc in next 2 dc, * ch 2, dc in next 3 dc, ch 4, sc in 4th ch from hook (p made), dc in next 3 dc. Repeat from * around. Join. **9th rnd:** Ch 3, dc in next 2 dc, * ch 2, dc in next 3 dc, ch 1, p, ch 1, dc in next 3 dc. Repeat from * around. Join. **10th rnd:** Ch 3, dc in next 2 dc, * ch 2, dc in next 3 dc, ch 2, p, ch 2, dc in next 3 dc. Repeat from * around. Join. **11th rnd:**

Ch 3, dc in next 2 dc, * ch 2, dc in next 3 dc, ch 11, dc in next 3 dc. Repeat from * around. Join. **12th rnd:** Ch 3, dc in next 2 dc, * ch 2, dc in next 3 dc, 11 dc in next sp, dc in next 3 dc. Repeat from * around. Join and fasten off.

Make necessary number of motifs and sew corresponding (9 dc, ch 2 and 9 dc) sides of adjacent motifs together with neat over-and-over sts on wrong side. There will be one group of 8 dc, ch 2 and 8 dc free between joinings.

FILL-IN-MOTIF . . . Ch 7, join. **1st rnd:** Ch 3, 15 dc in ring. Join with sl st to top st of ch-3. **2nd rnd:** Ch 7, * skip 1 dc, dc in next dc, ch 4. Repeat from * around, joining last ch-4 with sl st to 3rd st of ch-7 (8 sps). **3rd rnd:** Sl st in sp, ch 3, 7 dc in same sp, 8 dc in each following sp around. Join and fasten off.

Sew 8 dc (in sp of Fill-in-motif) to center 3 dc, ch 2 and 3 dc of free group of large motif. Sew 3 adjacent groups in this manner, leaving 4 groups of 8 dc free on Fill-in-motif. Fill all spaces between joinings in same way. Block to measurements given.

VALENTINE

(Continued from page 7)

Cut a piece of linen, 4¾ inches in diameter. Make a narrow hem around linen and make 240 sc closely all around outer edge. Join.

SHAMROCK EDGE . . . 1st rnd: Sc in same place as sl st, * (ch 2, picot) twice; ch 8, sl st in 6th ch from hook (this ch-6 loop is center of shamrock), turn, (ch 5, sc in center loop) 3 times; turn, in each of last three ch-5 loops make sc, 9 dc and sc; sc in ch-6 loop at center of Shamrock, ch 2, picot, ch 1, sc between the first and second picots, ch 2, picot, ch 2, skip 4 sc, sc in next sc, (ch 2, picot) twice; ch 2, skip 4 sc, sc in next sc. Repeat from * around (24 shamrocks). Break off. **2nd rnd:** Attach thread to 7th dc of first petal (counting from stem), (ch 2, picot) 3 times; ch 2, sc in center of 2nd petal, * (ch 2, picot) 3 times; ch 2, sc in 3rd dc on 3rd petal, ch 2, tr in next loop on center, ch 2, sc in 7th dc on first petal of

next shamrock, ch 2, picot, ch 1, turn and work sc between first and second picots of last picot-chain, turn, (ch 2, picot) twice; ch 2, sc in center of 2nd petal. Repeat from * around.

Join Edging to center as follows: Sl st to center of first loop, ch 2, picot, ch 1, sc in a loop on Edging, * ch 2, picot, ch 2, sc in next loop on center, ch 2, picot, ch 1, sc in next loop on Edging. Repeat from * around. Break off.

Now work along outer edge of Centerpiece as follows: Attach thread to joining of flowers, * ch 2, picot, ch 2, tr in next loop, ch 2, picot, ch 6, insert hook in 2nd ch from hook and draw loop through, (thread over, insert hook under same chain and draw loop through) 10 times; thread over and draw through all loops on hook, ch 1, sl st in next ch to hold strands tightly in place (clones knot made), ch 2, picot, ch 2, tr in same loop as last tr was made, ch 2, picot, ch 2, sc in next loop. Repeat from * around. Join and break off.

RUNNER . . . Make 18 Roses and 18 Thistles as for Edging, joining them in alternate order as for Centerpiece.

Now work around inner edge as for Centerpiece. Lay this piece aside. Cut a piece of linen 5¾ by 32 inches, rounding ends to form oval. Roll a narrow hem all around. Make sc closely around linen (17 sc to 1 inch). Join and break off.

Fold rounded end of linen down 2½ inches, place a pin as marker on each edge of linen at fold. Mark other rounded end in same way.

SHAMROCK EDGE . . . 1st rnd: Attach thread to first sc following marker and work around rounded end to next marker as for first rnd of Shamrock Edge of Centerpiece, being sure that there are 13 shamrocks between markers. Continue to work in pattern along straight edge to next marker, skipping necessary number of sc to keep work flat and having 23 shamrocks on side. Complete other rounded end and side to correspond (72 shamrocks in all). Join and break off. **2nd rnd:** Work as for 2nd rnd of Shamrock Edge on Centerpiece.

Join Edging to center as for Centerpiece. Now work along outer edges of Runner as for Centerpiece.

Starch each piece lightly and press.

Irish Crochet . . . to Cherish Forever

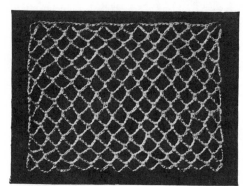

BACKGROUND No. 1

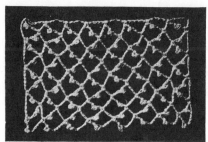

BACKGROUND No. 2

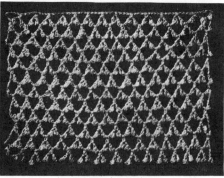

BACKGROUND No. 3

Background meshes used in Irish Crochet.

BACKGROUND No. 1

Make a ch a trifle longer than needed, s c in 10th st from hook, * ch 6, skip 3 sts, s c in next st, repeat from * to end of row, ch 8, turn.

2nd Row. S c in next loop, * ch 6, s c in next loop, repeat from * to end of row, ch 8, turn and repeat 2nd row.

BACKGROUND No. 2

Ch a little longer than desired, s c in 3rd st from hook, (this forms the picot) ch 2, s c in 9th ch from picot, * ch 5, picot, ch 2, skip 4 chs, s c in next ch (a single picot loop). Repeat from *, ch 9, turn.

2nd Row. Picot, ch 2, s c in next loop, * a single picot loop, s c in next loop, repeat from * and repeat 2nd row.

BACKGROUND No. 3

Chain a trifle longer than desired, ch 3, s c in 3rd st from hook, (this forms a picot) ch 1, picot, ch 1, s c in 4th ch from first picot * ch 1, picot, ch 1, picot, ch 1, skip 3 chs,

s c in next ch, (a double picot loop), repeat from * across row, ch 5, turn.

2nd Row. * Picot, ch 1, picot, ch 1, s c between picots of next loop, ch 1, repeat from * ending with s c between picots of last loop, repeat 2nd row.

IRISH CROCHET ROSE

Ch 7, join to form a ring, ch 6, d c into ring, * ch 3, d c into ring, repeat from * 3 times, ch 3 and join in 3rd st of ch 6 at beginning of row.

2nd Row. In each loop work 1 s c, 1 s d c, 3 d c, 1 s d c, and 1 s c.

3rd Row. * Ch 5, s c in back of work between the single crochets of next 2 petals, repeat from * all around.

4th Row. In each loop work 1 s c, 1 s d c, 5 d c, 1 s d c, 1 s c.

5th Row. * Ch 7, s c in back of work between next 2 petals, repeat from * all around.

6th Row. In each loop work 1 s c, 1 s d c, 7 d c, 1 s d c, 1 s c. Sl st in 1st s c of row and fasten thread.

MOTIF

Ch 5, join to form a ring.

2nd Row. Ch 6, d c in ring, * ch 3, d c in ring, repeat from * twice.

3rd Row. Ch 1, * 1 d c, 7 tr c, 1 d c in ch 3, 1 s c in d c, repeat from * all around.

4th Row. * Ch 6, s c in next s c in back of petal, repeat from * all around.

5th Row. S c in s c, * 1 d c, 8 tr c, 1 d c in loop, s c in s c, repeat from * all around.

6th Row. Sl st to 2nd tr c, * ch 7, sl st in 5th st from hook for picot, ch 7, sl st in 5th st from hook for picot, ch 2, skip 4 tr c, s c in next tr c make another double picot loop, and s c in 2nd tr c of next petal, repeat from * all around.

7th Row. Sl st to center of loop between picot, * double

(Continued on page 44)

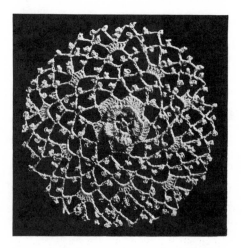

Placemats with Rose Border

This set may be made with any of the
AMERICAN THREAD COMPANY products listed below:

Material	Quantity	Size of
"GEM" CROCHET COTTON	5 balls Shaded Pinks	Needle
Article 35, size 30	4 balls Nile Green	steel 12
or		
"STAR" CROCHET COTTON	6 balls Shaded Pinks	steel 12
Article 20, size 30	4 balls Nile Green	
or		
"STAR" CROCHET COTTON	15 balls Shaded Pinks	steel 12
Article 30, size 30	10 balls Nile Green	

Finished mats measure 10 inches x 18¼ inches.
1½ yds. 35 inch Gray linen will make 4 place mats and 4 napkins.
Each flower measures 1¼ inches.
Inside of crocheted section should measure 10 inches x 16½ inches.

PLACE MAT—ROSE: With Shaded Pinks ch 5, join to form a ring, ch 5, d c in ring, * ch 2, d c in ring, repeat from * 5 times, ch 2, join in 3rd st of ch.

2nd Row—Ch 1 and over each loop work 1 s c, 4 d c, 1 s c, join.
3rd Row—* Ch 5, sl st in back of work between next 2 petals, repeat from * all around.
4th Row—Ch 1 and over each loop work 1 s c, 7 d c, 1 s c, join.
5th Row—* Ch 6, sl st in back of work between next 2 petals, repeat from * all around, cut thread.
6th Row—Attach Nile Green in loop and work 1 s c, 1 d c, 5 tr c, 1 d c, 1 s c in each loop, join, cut thread.
Work a 2nd flower joining it to 1st flower in last row as follows: attach Green in loop, 1 s c, 1 d c, 3 tr c in same space, join to center st of any Green petal of 1st flower (to join: drop loop off hook, insert in center st of petal, pick up loop and pull through), 2 tr c, 1 d c, 1 s c in same space, 1 s c, 1 d c, 3 tr c in next loop of 2nd flower, join to next petal of 1st flower, 2 tr c, 1 d c, 1 s c in same space of 2nd flower, finish row same as 1st flower. Work 13 more flowers joining in same manner leaving 2 petals free at top and 2 petals free at lower edge between joinings. Last flower made will be corner flower.

(Continued on page 44)

11

No. 8879 . . . Make a chain 1¼ times longer than length desired. **1st row:** Sc in 2nd ch from hook, * ch 10, skip 7 ch, sc in next ch. Repeat from * until 1st row is desired length, having a multiple of 3 plus 2 loops. Cut off remaining chain. Ch 1, turn. **2nd row:** * 7 sc in next loop, ch 10, sc in next loop, ch 1, turn. Make 14 sc over ch-10 loop, sl st in next sc. Ch 1, turn; sc in 14 sc. Turn; (ch 7, skip 4 sc, sc in next sc) twice; ch 7, sc in sl st. Ch 1, turn. In each ch-7 loop make sc, h dc, 7 dc, h dc and sc, sl st in next sc. Make 7 sc in same loop on 1st row, 7 sc in next loop, ch 8, sc in 8th ch from hook, (ch 7, sc in same place as last sc) twice; 7 sc in same loop. Repeat from * across. Fasten off.

Heading . . . With right side facing, attach thread to end of foundation chain. Ch 3, dc in same place, ch 6, sc in each of next 2 loops, * ch 6, dc in same loop as last dc, dc in next loop. Repeat from * across. Fasten off.

No. 8846 . . . First Flower . . . Ch 8, join with sl st to form ring. **1st rnd:** Ch 3, 2 dc in ring, (ch 5, sc in 3rd ch from hook, ch 2, 3 dc in ring) 6 times; ch 5, sc in 3rd ch from hook, ch 2, sl st in top st of ch-3. **2nd rnd:** Sc in next dc, (ch 10, sc in center dc of next

group) 6 times; ch 10, sl st in 1st sc. Fasten off.

Second Flower . . . Work as for 1st flower until 1st rnd is complete. **2nd rnd:** Sc in next dc, ch 5, sc in any ch-10 loop on 1st flower, ch 5, sc in center dc of next group on 2nd flower. Finish 2nd rnd as before (no more joinings). Fasten off.

Make necessary number of flowers, joining them as 2nd was joined to 1st, having two ch-10 loops free on upper edge and 3 loops free on lower edge.

Heading . . . With right side facing, attach thread in 2nd loop to the right of 1st joining. **1st row:** Ch 1, sc in same place where thread was attached, * ch 5, sc in next loop, ch 5, holding back last loop of each d tr on hook make d tr in each of next 2 (joined) loops, thread over and draw through all loops on hook, ch 5, sc in next loop on next flower. Repeat from * across. Ch 9, turn. **2nd row:** * Dc in next sc, ch 5. Repeat from * across. Fasten off.

No. 8878 . . . Make a chain 1½ times longer than length desired. **1st row:** Sc in 2nd ch from hook and in each ch across until 1st row is desired length, having a multiple of 20 plus 9 sc's. Cut off remaining chain. Ch 1, turn. **2nd row:** Sc in 1st sc, * ch 7, skip

3 sc, sc in next sc, (ch 7, skip 3 sc, sc in next 5 sc) twice. Repeat from * across, ending with (ch 7, skip 3 sc, sc in next sc) twice. Ch 1, turn. **3rd row:** * In next loop make (3 sc, ch 3, sc in 3rd ch from hook — *p made*) twice and 3 sc; in next loop make 3 sc, p, 1 sc, ch 10, turn, sl st in center sc (between p's) of last loop, turn. In ch-10 loop make (3 sc, p) 3 times and 3 sc; make 1 sc, p and 3 sc in last ch-7 loop, skip 1 sc, sc in next 3 sc, in next loop make (3 sc, p) twice and 3 sc; skip 1 sc, sc in next 3 sc. Repeat from * across. Fasten off.

No. 8871 . . . Make a chain 1½ times longer than length desired. **1st row:** Sc in 2nd ch from hook, sc in next 6 ch, * ch 7, skip 4 ch, sc in next 7 ch. Repeat from * across until 1st row is length desired. Cut off remaining chain. Ch 1, turn. **2nd row:** Skip 1st sc, sc in next 5 sc, * ch 5, sc in loop. Ch 5, skip next sc, sc in next 5 sc. Repeat from * across. Ch 1, turn. **3rd row:** Skip 1st sc, sc in next 3 sc, * ch 7, skip next sc, sc in next sc, ch 7, skip next sc, sc in next 3 sc. Repeat from * across. Ch 1, turn. **4th row:** Skip 1st sc, sc in next sc, * ch 5, sc in next loop, (ch 3, sc in 3rd ch from hook) 3 times; sc in next loop, ch 5, skip 1 sc, sc in next sc. Repeat from * across. Fasten off.

CRISP FINISHES
FOR YOUR CHOICEST
HANKIES OR DAINTY
COLLARS AND CUFFS

No. 8857 . . . Starting at narrow end, ch 5, sl st in 5th ch from hook. Ch 7, turn. **1st row:** 3 dc in ch-5 loop. Ch 5, turn, sc in top of 1st dc made. Ch 7, turn. Repeat 1st row for length desired, having an even number of ch-7 loops and ending with **3** dc. Ch 5, turn and work scalloped edge as follows: **1st row:** * Tr in next ch-7 loop, ch 3, holding back the last loop of each tr on hook make 3 tr in same ch-7 loop, thread over and draw through all loops on hook (cluster made), ch 3, tr in same ch-7 loop, dc in next loop. Repeat from * across, ending with dc in last loop. Ch 3, turn. **2nd row:** * In tip of next cluster, make 3 clusters with ch 4 between, tr in next dc. Repeat from * across, ending with 3 clusters. Ch 1, turn. **3rd row:** Sc in tip of 1st cluster, * ch 5, dc in tip of center cluster of group, ch 5, sc in next tr. Repeat from * across, ending with ch 5, sc in tip of last cluster. Ch 8, turn. **4th row:** * Dc in next dc, ch 5, dc in next sc, ch 5. Repeat from * across, ending with dc in last sc. Ch 8, turn. **5th row:** * In next dc make dc, ch 3, sc in 3rd ch from hook and dc; ch 5, dc in next dc, ch 5. Repeat from * across, ending with ch 5, dc in 4th st of turning ch. Fasten off.

No. 8848 . . . Make a chain slightly longer than desired. **1st row:** Sc in 2nd ch from hook, * ch 7, skip 9 ch, in next ch make 2 tr with ch 17 between, ch 7, skip 9 ch, sc in next ch. Repeat from * across. Ch 1, turn. **2nd row:** * 5 sc in next loop, ch 3, 15 dc in next sp, ch 3, 5 sc in next loop. Repeat from * across. Ch 1, turn. **3rd row:** Skip 1st sc, * sc in 4 sc, ch 3, dc in next dc, (ch 2, skip 1 dc, dc in next dc) 7 times; ch 3, sc in next 4 sc, skip 2 sc. Repeat from * across. **4th row:** Skip 1st sc, * sc in 3 sc, ch 5, sc in ch-2 sp, (ch 5, sc in 3rd ch from hook, ch 2, sc in next sp) 6 times; ch 5, sc in next 3 sc, skip 2 sc. Repeat from * across. Fasten off.

No. 8928 . . . Make a chain slightly longer than length desired. **1st row:** Dc in 4th ch from hook and in next 3 ch, * ch 5, skip 5 ch, dc in next ch, ch 5, skip 5 ch, dc in next 9 ch. Repeat from * across for length desired, ending with 5 dc. Ch 3, turn. Cut off remaining chain. **2nd row:** Dc in next 3 dc, * ch 5, skip next sp, 3 dc in next dc, ch 5, skip next sp, dc in next 7 dc. Repeat from * across, ending with 4 dc. Ch 3, turn. **3rd row:** Dc in next 2 dc, * ch 5, skip next sp, 3 dc in each of next 3 dc, ch 5, skip 1 dc, dc in next 5 dc. Repeat from * across, ending with 3 dc. Ch 3, turn. **4th row:** Dc in next dc, * ch 5, skip next sp, dc in next 4 dc, ch 3, skip 1 dc, dc in next 4 dc, ch 5, skip 1 dc, dc in next 3 dc. Repeat from * across, ending with 2 dc. Ch 8, turn. **5th row:** Skip next sp, then holding back on hook the last loop of each dc, work dc in each of next 4 dc, thread over and draw through all loops on hook (cluster made), * ch 3, 5 dc in next sp, ch 3, cluster over next 4 dc, ch 5, skip 1 dc, dc in next dc, ch 5, cluster over next 4 dc. Repeat from * across, ending with ch 5, dc in top of turning ch. Ch 1, turn. **6th row:** 5 sc in sp, * sc in tip of cluster, ch 7, then holding back on hook the last loop of each tr work tr in each of next 5 dc and complete cluster as before, (ch 5, sc in tip of cluster) 3 times; ch 7, sc in tip of next cluster, 5 sc in each of next 2 sps. Repeat from * across. Fasten off.

No. 8881... Motif—Center Flower . . . Starting at center, ch 10, join with sl st to form ring. **1st rnd:** Ch 1, work 20 sc in ring. Join with sl st in 1st sc. **2nd rnd:** Ch 1, sc in same place as sl st, * ch 5, skip 3 sc, sc in next sc. Repeat from * around. Join last ch-5 with sl st in 1st sc. **3rd rnd:** In each loop around make sc, h dc, 5 dc, h dc and sc. Join. **4th rnd:** * Ch 5, sc between sc's of next 2 petals. Repeat from * around. Join. **5th rnd:** Make a petal in each loop, having 7 dc instead of 5 dc on each petal. Fasten off.

Motif . . . Starting at center, ch 15. Join with sl st to form ring. **1st rnd:** Ch 1, work 26 sc in ring. Join with sl st in 1st sc. **2nd rnd:** Ch 4, * dc in next sc, ch 1. Repeat from * around. Join to 3rd st of ch-4 first made (26 sps). **3rd rnd:** 2 sc in each sp around. Join (52 sc). **4th rnd:** Ch 4, tr in each sc around, increasing 8 tr

(Continued on page 44)

13

Edgings for That Special Gift

WE SUGGEST ROYAL SOCIETY CORDICHET, SIZE 30

No. 3-10 . . . FIRST MOTIF . . .
Ch 6, join with sl st to form ring.
1st rnd: Ch 1, 16 sc in ring. Join with
sl st in 1st sc. **2nd rnd:** Ch 9 (to count
as tr and ch 5), * sk 1 sc, tr in next sc,
ch 5. Repeat from * around. Join last
ch-5 with sl st in 4th st of starting
chain. **3rd rnd:** Ch 1, sc in same place
as sl st, * 5 sc in next sp, sc in next tr.
Repeat from * around. Join. **4th rnd:**
Ch 1, sc in same place at sl st, * ch 10,
sk 5 sc, sc in next sc. Repeat from *
around. Join. **5th rnd:** Make 15 sc in
each loop around. Join and fasten off.
SECOND MOTIF . . . Work as for
1st motif to 4th rnd inclusive. **5th
rnd:** * 7 sc in next loop, sl st in 8th
st of a 15-sc loop on 1st motif, being
careful to keep right side of each
motif uppermost, 7 sc in same loop
on 2nd motif. Repeat from * once
more. Complete rnd as for 1st motif.
Fasten off. Make and join necessary
number of motifs for length desired.

HEADING . . . 1st row: With right
side facing, attach thread to the 8th
st on 3rd loop (from joining on 1st
motif), ch 1, sc in same place where
thread was attached, ch 13, sc in 8th
sc of next loop of same motif, * ch 8,
sc in 8th sc of next loop of same
motif, ch 8, d tr in joining of motifs,
ch 8, sc in 8th sc of next loop of next
motif. Repeat from * across, ending
with d tr in 8th st of 3rd loop (from
joining on last motif). Ch 5, turn. **2nd
row:** * (Sk 2 ch, dc in next ch, ch 2)
twice; dc in next st, ch 2. Repeat
from * across. Fasten off.

No. 3-11 . . . Starting at narrow end,
ch 9. **1st row:** Dc in 6th ch from hook,
dc in next 3 ch. Ch 5, turn. **2nd row:**
Dc in 4 dc. Ch 5, turn. Repeat 2nd
row until piece is longer than desired,
having a multiple of 18 plus 5 dc
groups. Do not fasten off as the 1st

row of heading will determine the ac-
tual length and more may have to be
added.

HEADING . . . 1st row: Attach another strand of thread in second ch-5
sp from beginning of piece, ch 1, sc
in same sp, ch 3, sc in next sp, * ch 3,
holding back the last loop of each dc
on hook make 2 dc in next sp, thread
over and draw through all loops on
hook (2-dc cluster made); ch 3, make
a 2-tr cluster in next sp, ch 3, make a
2-d tr cluster in next sp, ch 3, make a
2-tr tr cluster in next sp, ch 3, a 2-d tr
cluster in next sp, ch 3, a 2-tr cluster in next sp, ch 3, a 2-dc cluster in
next sp, (ch 3, sc in next sp) twice.
Repeat from * across, ending with sc
in last 2 loops with ch-3 between. Ch
4, turn. **2nd row:** * Dc in next sp,
ch 1, dc in top of next st, ch 1. Repeat
from * across. Fasten off.

SCALLOPS . . . With right side of
heading facing, attach thread in 1st

14

sp on opposite edge of piece, ch 1, sc in same place where thread was attached, sc in each of next 2 loops, ** ch 1, * tr in next sp, ch 3, sc in 3rd ch from hook (p made), tr in same sp, p, tr in same sp. Repeat from * 5 more times; ch 1, sc in each of the next 3 sps. Repeat from * * across. Fasten off.

No. 3-12 . . . Make a chain 1½ times longer than length desired. **1st row:** Dc in 6th ch from hook, * ch 1, sk 1 ch, dc in next ch. Repeat from * until 1st row is desired length, having a multiple of 9 plus 3 sps. Turn. **2nd row:** Sl st in 1st sp, ch 1, sc in same sp, * ch 10, sk 1 sp, sc in next sp, turn. In ch-10 loop make (sc, h dc, dc, h dc) 4 times and sc. Ch 10, turn. Dc in dc of 2nd scallop, ch 7, dc in dc of next scallop. Ch 10, sc in original ch-10 loop, turn. Work 10 sc over next loop, 11 sc over center loop and 10 sc over last loop, sl st in original ch-10 loop. Ch 1, turn. Sc in 2 sc, ch 3, sc in 3rd ch from hook (p made), (sc in next 3 sc, p) 9 times; sc in last 2 sc. Then work (sc in next dc, sc in next sp) 7 times. Repeat from * until the sc's are worked over each of the 3 loops, sl st in original ch-10 loop. Ch 1, turn. Sc in 2 sc, p, sc in 3 sc, ch 1, sc in next to the last p on last scallop, ch 1, sc in 1st ch-1 of this p, sc in next 3 sc on 2nd scallop and continue as for 1st scallop until all the sps have been worked over. Fasten off.

HEADING . . . With wrong side of 1st row facing, attach thread in 1st sp, ch 4, sk 2 sps, holding back the last loop of each tr on hook make 3 tr in next sp, thread over and draw through all loops on hook (3-tr cluster made), * ch 7, sk 1 sp, holding back the last loop of each dc on hook make 3 dc in next sp, complete cluster (3-dc cluster made), ch 7, sk 1 sp, 3-tr cluster in next sp, sk 4 sps, 3-tr cluster in next sp. Repeat from * across, ending with ch 4, sc in last sp. Fasten off.

No. 3-13 . . . **EDGING** . . . Starting at one narrow end, ch 10. **1st row:** Dc in 6th ch from hook, (ch 1, sk 1 ch, dc in next ch) twice. Ch 4, turn. **2nd row:** Dc in next dc, ch 1, dc in next dc, ch 1, sk 1 ch, dc in next ch, ch 4, then holding back the last loop of each tr on hook work 2 tr in last dc, thread over and draw through all loops on hook (cluster made). Ch 9, turn. **3rd row:** Dc in 6th ch from hook, ch 1, sk 1 ch, dc in next ch, ch 1, dc in top of cluster. Ch 4, turn.

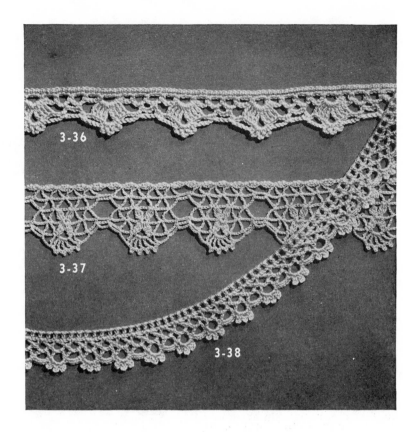

Repeat the 2nd and 3rd rows alternately for length desired, ending with 3rd row. Do not fasten off but ch 4 to turn and work as follows: **Next row:** Dc in next dc, ch 1, dc in next dc, ch 1, sk 1 ch, dc in next ch, ch 7 and continue along length of edging. Sk 1 sp, * in next sp work three 3-tr clusters with ch-5 between, sk 2 sps, next cluster and 1 sp. Repeat from * across, ending with ch 7, sl st in 1st ch at beginning of edging. Do not fasten off but sl st to top of dc and in next 2 ch, then work along top as follows:

HEADING . . . Sc in sp, ch 4, then holding back the last loop of each tr on hook work 2 tr in same sp and complete a cluster as before, * sk 2 sps, work d tr under ch-4 of next cluster, ch 7, d tr in same place, sk 1 sp, 3-tr cluster in next sp. Repeat from * across. Fasten off.

INSERTION . . . **1st, 2nd and 3rd rows:** Same as for Edging. Repeat the 2nd and 3rd rows alternately for length desired, ending with 3rd row. Do not fasten off but ch 4 to turn and work as follows: **Next row:** Dc in next dc, ch 1, dc in next dc, ch 4, sk 1 ch, sl st in next 2 ch, then follow directions for Heading. Fasten off. Attach thread and work Heading along other long edge in same way.

No. 3-36 . . . Make a chain 1¼ times longer than desired. **1st row:** Sc in 2nd ch from hook and in each ch across. Ch 1, turn. **2nd row:** Sc in next sc, * ch 4, sk 2 sc, sc in next sc. Repeat from * until row is desired length, being sure there is a multiple of 5 plus 1 loops. Cut and fasten off remainder of piece. Turn. **3rd row:** Sl st in 1st loop, ch 4, in same loop make 3 tr, ch 3 and 4 tr, * ch 4, sk 1 loop, sc in next loop, ch 4, sc in next loop, ch 4, sk 1 loop, in next loop make 4 tr, ch 3 and 4 tr. Repeat from * across. Ch 5, turn. **4th row:** In ch-3 sp make (sc, ch 3) 3 times and sc; * ch 5, sc in next loop, ch 4, sk next loop, sc in next loop, ch 5, in next ch-3 sp make (sc, ch 3) 3 times and sc. Repeat from * across, ending with ch 5, sl st in top st of turning ch. Fasten off.

No. 3-37 . . . Starting at narrow end, ch 5. **1st row:** Holding back the last loop of each tr on hook make 2 tr in 5th ch from hook, thread over and draw through all loops on hook, ch 1 to fasten (a 3-tr cluster made). **2nd row:** Ch 4, holding back the last loop of each tr on hook make 2 tr in fastening ch of last cluster, complete cluster as before. Repeat 2nd row for

(Continued on page 45)

15

Clover Leaf Doily

MATERIALS — DAISY Mercerized Crochet Cotton size 30:—A partial ball White, Cream or Ecru. Crochet hook size 12. Size—13½″. Starting with the row of clover leaves around the lacy center, ch 12, sl st in 1st st. Ch 1, turn, (4 sc in ring, ch 5, sl st in last sc for a p) 3 times, 4 sc in ring, ** ch 48, remove hook from lp and insert it back in 12th st from hook, catch lp and pull thru, ch 1, 16 sc in ring, turn, (ch 18, sk 3 sc on ring, sc in next 3 sc) twice, ch 18, sk 3 sc, sl st in end sc. Ch 1, turn, 2 sc and 2 hdc in 18-ch lp, (3 dc in lp, a p) 3 times and 3 dc in lp sl st back in last p on previous ring, being careful that long ch is not twisted. (3 dc, p, 3 dc, 2 hdc and 2 sc) in bal. of lp, * sl st in center sc between petals, 2 sc and 2 hdc in next lp, (3 dc, p) 5 times in lp, (3 dc, 2 hdc and 2 sc) in lp. Repeat from * once. Sl st on left side of center ring to draw top together, 5 sc on stem ch, ch 42, remove hook, insert it back in 12th ch st, catch lp and pull thru, ch 1, 4 sc in ring, sk last 3 ps on clover leaf, sl st back in next p, (4 sc, p, 4 sc, p and 4 sc) in bal. of ring. Repeat from ** thru 8th clover leaf, joining 1st and last motifs to form a circle with clover leaves pointing toward center. Ch 30, sl st across in starting st at base of 1st ring. (5 sc, p) 6 times and 5 sc in each large lp around outside of circle. Fasten off. **ROW 2**—Join to 3d p on next lp, * ch 14, a 4-dtr-Cluster in next p, ch 14, sc in next p, ch 12, sc in 2d p on next lp, ch 14, a Cluster in next p, ch 14, sc in next p, ch 14, sc in 3d p on next lp. Repeat from * around. **ROW 3**—* (4 sc, p) 3 times and 4 sc in next lp, ch 9, a 3-dtr-Cluster in 9th ch st from hook, a p, ch 8, sl st at base of Cluster, (4 sc, p) 3 times and 4 sc in next lp, ** (6 sc, p, 6 sc) in next lp. Repeat from * to **. (7 sc, p, 7 sc) in next lp. Repeat from * around. Fasten off. **ROW 4**—Join to tip of next Cluster, ch 12, dc in same p, * ch 14, a 4-dtr-Cluster in next 2d p, ch 9, a Cluster in next 4th p, ch 14, (dc, ch 9, dc) in next Cluster. Repeat from * around. Join to 3d st of 1st 12-ch lp. **ROW 5**—5 sc in next lp, ch 18 and form a ring as before in 12th st from hook, ch 1, 16 sc in ring, turn, (ch 18, sk last 3 sc, sc in next 3 sc) twice, ch 18, sl st in end sc. Ch 1, turn, * 2 sc and 2 hdc in 18-ch lp, (3 dc, p) 5 times in lp, (3 dc, 2 hdc and 2 sc) in lp, sl st between petals. Repeat from * twice. Sl st on left side of center ring, 5 sc on stem, 5 sc in bal. of next lp, (4 sc, p) 3 times and 4 sc in next lp, (5 sc, p, 5 sc) in next lp, (4 sc,

p) 3 times and 4 sc in next lp. Repeat from beginning of row around. Fasten off.

EDGE—Join to 2d p on center petal of one leaf, * ch 20, sc in next 2d p, ch 25, sc in 3d p on next petal, ch 11, tr down in center p between leaves, ch 11, sc in 3d p on next leaf, ch 25, sc in 2d p on next petal. Repeat from * around. **ROW 2**—* (6 sc, p) 3 times and 6 sc in next lp, (5 sc, p) 5 times and 5 sc in next lp, (12 sc in next lp) twice, 5 sc in next, ch 2, sl st back in last p, ch 2, sl st back in last sc to complete p, (5 sc, p) 4 times and 5 sc in bal. of lp. Repeat from * around. Fasten off.

CENTER—Ch 12, sl st in 1st st. Ch 1, 16 sc in ring. In back lps, sl st in 1st sc, * ch 8, a 3-dtr-Cluster in same st, a p, ch 8, sl st in same sc, sl st in next 2 sc. Repeat from * 7 times. Fasten off. **ROW 2**—Join to one petal, ch 12 dc in same p, * ch 15, (dc, ch 9, dc) in next petal. Repeat from * 6 times. Ch 8, dtr in 3d st of 1st 12-ch. **ROW 3**—(Ch 15, sc in next lp) 15 times, ch 8, dtr in next lp. **ROW 4**—* Ch 14, sc in 5th st from hook for a p, (ch 6, p) 3 times, ch 3, sl st in ring between 2 leaves, ch 7, p, dc between last 2 ps, (ch 5, p, dc between next 2 ps) twice, ch 5, p, ch 2, sl st in 2d st past next p, ch 7, sc in next lp, ch 9, sl st in center p of leaf, ch 9, sc back in next lp. Repeat from * around. Fasten off.

Pin right-side-down in a true circle, stretching several inches. Steam and press dry thru a cloth.

Crocheted Medallions

Ch 10, join in ring, * in ring work 1 s c, 5 d c, 1 s c, repeat 3 more times from *. **2d rnd:** Ch 6, s c in 3d d c, ch 6, s c between petals, repeat around. Join with sl st. 8 loops in rnd. **3d rnd:** In each loop make 1 s c, 7 d c, 1 s c. **4th rnd:** Sl st to 2d d c and in it make 1 s c. * Ch 10, s c in 5th d c of same petal, ch 10, s c in center d c of next petal. Ch 10, s c in 2d d c of next petal. Repeat from * around, 12 loops in rnd. **5th rnd:** Sl st to center of 1st loop. * Ch 8, s c in next loop, turn, 10 s c over ch-8, turn, s c in each s c, turn, ch 6, s c in 3d s c, ch 6, skip 3 s c, 1 s c in next, ch 6, 1 s c in last s c. Turn, in each ch-6 loop make 1 s c, 7 d c, 1 s c. Ch 10, s c in next loop of preceding rnd, ch 10, s c in next loop. Repeat from * around. Fasten last ch-10 to 1st s c of rnd. Turn and sl st back to center of ch-10 last made. **6th rnd:** Turn, s c in center of loop (where sl st ends), ch 10, s c in center of 1st petal, ch 10, s c in 2d d c of 2d petal, ch 10, s c in 6th d c of same petal, ch 10, s c in center next petal, ch 10, s c in next loop, ch 10, s c in next loop. Repeat around. **7th rnd:** 5 s c, p, 5 s c in each loop.

Ch 6, join in a ring. Ch 8, * d c in ring, ch 5, repeat from * until 5 d c have been made in ring, ch 5. Join last ch-5 to 3d st of starting ch of rnd. 6 sps in rnd. **2d rnd:** In each sp make 1 s c, 1 half d c, 1 d c, 3 tr, 1 d c, 1 half d c, 1 s c. Join. **3d rnd:** Sl st to 1st d c of 1st scallop. * Ch 7, catch in 5th ch from hook for a p, ch 8 and catch for p, ch 2, s c in next d c of same scallop. Make loop with 2 p as before, s c in 1st d c of next scallop, and repeat from *. Join last loop to 1st s c of rnd. 12 loops in rnd. **4th rnd:** Sl st to center of 1st loop, working behind p. S c under center of loop, * ch 7, s c under center of next loop. Turn, ch 7, catch where 1st ch-7 started. Ch 3, turn, 9 d c under double ch-7. Ch 3, s c in center of loop where s c after 1st ch-7 was made. Make 2 p loops as in preceding rnd, working s c under center of loops below. Repeat from * around. Catch down last loop in s c with which round started. 4 d c shells in round, always with 2 p loops between shells. **5th rnd:** Sl st to top of 1st d c of 1st shell. Work 1 s c in same d c. Work p loops all around catching down in beginning, end, and center of each d c shell, and in each p loop of preceding round. Catch down last loop in s c with which rnd started. **6th rnd:** Sl st to center of 1st loop. Over each shell of 4th rnd make same shell and between shells work 4 p loops. Make 2 rnds all p loops, working as instructed for 5th rnd.

Killarney Bedspread

A Novel, New Spread in Irish Crochet.

Lacy Edges Add Distinction.

MATERIALS: Lily Mills "Daisy Thread," in White, No. 10 No. 7 hook.

BLOCK—Border: Ch 10, sk last 2 ch sts, 1 sc in remaining 8 sts. (Ch 1, turn, 1 sc in each sc of last row) 7 times. * Ch 10, turn ch and previous Square over, wrong-side-up, sk last 2 ch sts, 1 sc in remaining 8 sts. (Ch 1, turn, 1 sc in each sc of last row) 7 times. * Repeat from * to * 4 times. * * Ch 18, sk last 2 ch sts, 1 sc in next 8 sts, sk next ch st, 1 sl st in next, (ch 1, turn, sk sl st, 1 sc in each of the 8-sc of last row, ch 1, turn, 1 sc in the 8-sc, 1 sl st under ch) 3 times, making final sl st in 1st st of 18-ch next to previous Square. This last row of sc and the final row on last Square should both be right-side-up when this final sl st is made. Ch 1, turn, 1 sc in 8 sc of last row. * * Repeat from * to * 5 times. Repeat from * * to * * for another corner Square. Ch 11, turn Square around, keeping same right-side up, remove hook from loop, insert in diagonally opposite corner, let 11-ch lie across back of Square, catch loop and pull thru. Repeat from * to * 5 times. Repeat from * * to * * for 3rd Corner Square. Then repeat from * to * 5 times. Turn and make a sl st in corner of 1st Square at starting end of 1st row of sc, completing the Border.

Heading Row: In this row, be very careful not to twist the Squares as the rows of sc in all Squares all around the Block, should all run in the same direction. Ch 5, 1 dc halfway along the side of same Corner Square, ch 6, 1 sc in corner, * * ch 6, 1 tr in center of next side of same Corner Square, ch 6, 1 sc in next corner, * ch 6, 1 dc in center of next side of same Square, 1 tr between Squares, 1 dc in center of side of next Square, remove hook from loop, insert in previous dc, catch loop and pull thru, drawing up group of 2 dc and tr tight, ch 6, 1 sc in next corner. Repeat from * 5 times. Then repeat from * * around Block. Finish row its 6-ch and a dc, 1 sl st in 1st dc in row. Fasten off.

CENTER OF BLOCK: Ch 8, join with a sl st into a ring, ch 6, 1 dc in next st of center ring, (ch 3, 1 dc in next st of ring) 6 times, ch 3, 1 sl st in 3rd st of 6-ch. **2nd ROW:** Ch 3, (4 dc over next 3-ch, 1 dc in dc) repeated around, 1 sl st in 3-ch at start. **3rd ROW:** * Ch 7, 3 d tr in same st holding the last loop of each d tr on hook, thread over and pull thru 2 loops, over and thru remaining 3 loops on hook, a 5-ch p in top of Cluster, (ch 5, 1 sc in 1st st for a p) 4 times, ch 3, 1 sl st in back loop of next 5th dc. Repeat from * 7 times. Fasten off. **4th ROW:** Join again to the 5-ch p at tip of 1 Cluster, * (ch 7, 1 sc in 5th st from hook for a 5-ch p) twice, ch 3, 1 d tr in 5-ch p at tip of next Cluster, (ch 6, a 5-ch p, ch 2, 1 d tr in same p) 4 times, (ch 7, a p) twice, ch 3, 1 sc in p at tip of next Cluster. Repeat from * 3 times. Fasten off. **5th ROW:** Join again to the center st between ps of last p-loop of last row, ch 3 in place of a dc, * ch 8, 1 sc in 5th st from hook for a 5-ch p, ch 4, 1 sl st in inside corner of Square on center of 1 side of Block Border, ch 8, p, ch 4, 1 dc in center st of next p-loop, ch 8, p, ch 4, 1 sl st in corner of next Square, ch 8, p, ch 4, sk next 2 d tr, 1 dc in next p, ch 8, p, ch 4, 1 sl st in corner of next Square, ch 8, p, ch 4, 1 sl st across Corner in corner of next Square, ch 8, p, ch 4, sk next d tr, 1 dc in next p, ch 8, p, ch 4, 1 sl st in corner of next Square, ch 8, p, ch 4, sk next 2 d tr, 1 dc in center st between ps of next p-loop. Repeat from * 3 times and fasten off, completing Block. On tissue paper, draw a true square slightly larger than finished Block. Stretch and pin Block right-side-down on this pattern on a well-padded ironing board and steam with a hot iron and wet cloth, then press thru a dry cloth until thoroughly dry. A Spread pressed in this way will hold its shape and flatness indefinitely.

Sew Blocks together, following diagram, going thru a single loop of each st. Be careful when joining Blocks that the rows of sc in all Blocks run in the same direction.

EDGE: Starting at beginning of "Block Border" directions, make 1 Square the same as the 1st Square of Border, then repeat from * to * 6 times. Then repeat from * * to * * once. Then repeat from * to * 7 times. * * * Then repeat from * * to * * once. Ch 11, turn Square around, keeping same side up, remove hook, insert in diagonally opposite corner, let 11-ch lie across back of Square, catch loop and pull thru. Repeat from * to * 6 times. Then repeat from * * to * * once. Turn work over, ch 11, remove hook, insert in diagonally opposite corner, let 11-ch lie across back of Square, catch loop and pull thru. Repeat from * to * 6 times. Repeat from * * * to next corner of Spread. Then go around that corner Block in same way as first one, and continue.

HEADING ROW: Make the same as the Heading Row around Blocks. When the outside corners of Corner Blocks are reached, ch 6, 1 dc in center of side of Square next to Corner Square, 1 tr between Squares, holding the last loop of each of these 2 sts on hook, thread over and pull thru all loops on hook at once, 1 dc in center of Corner Square, 1 tr between squares, and work these 2 sts off together as just explained, 1 dc in center of next Square, ch 6, 1 sc in corner of same Square. When completed, sew Heading Row of Edge to Heading Row of Blocks around edge of Spread.

2nd ROW of EDGE: Join to corner of 2nd Square around 1 Corner Block, (ch 8, 1 sc in 5th st from hook for a 5-ch p, ch 12, a 5-ch p, ch 4, 1 sc in corner of next square) 6 times, * ch 8, p, ch 4, 1 d tr in center of side of same Corner Square, ch 6, p, ch 2, 1 d tr in same place, ch 8, p, ch 4, 1 sc in next corner, * (ch 8, p, ch 12, p, ch 4, 1 sc in corner

(Continued on page 45)

19

Renaissance Collar

Materials: J. & P. Coats (2 balls) or Clark's O.N.T. (3 balls) Mercerized Crochet, size 60, White. Milward's steel crochet hook No. 10 or 11. 1 ball pearl button for fastening.

First Petal. Ch 25, turn. **1st row:** 1 s c in 6th ch from hook, 1 s c in each ch to end of row. Ch 5 and s c on other side of foundation in each st to within 2 s c from end. Ch 5, turn. **2nd row:** 1 s c (always picking up only back loop of s c's) in each s c of previous row, 3 s c under ch-5 loop, ch 5, 3 s c under same loop, 1 s c in each s c to within 2 s c from end. Ch 5, turn. Repeat 2nd row until there are 20 ch-5 loops, ch 9, turn. **Next row:** * 1 s c in 7th s c from hook, ch 9, and repeat from * all around, making the s c's in the ch-5 loops at bottom sides, ending row with 1 s c under top ch-5 loop, ch 5, turn. **Last row:** 1 s c in first ch-9 loop, * ch 4, ch-5 p, ch 5, 1 s c in same place as last s c, ch 5, 1 s c in same place, (3 p's made) ch 4, s c under next ch-9 loop, repeat from * around. Break thread.

Second Petal. Make this petal same as first petal to within last row. **Last row:** 1 s c in first ch-9 loop, ch 4, ch-5 p, ch 2, sl st in center p (at top) of first petal, * ch 2, s c back in same place as last s c on second petal, ch 5, s c in same place, ch 4, s c under next ch-9 loop of second petal, ch 4, ch-5 p, ch 2, sl st in center p of next 3-p group of first petal, repeat from * until 8 groups of p's (only on long sides of petals) are joined. Work remainder of this row as before, but without joining to previous petal.

Work 8 more petals and join each petal to previous one as second petal was joined to the first.

Heading. 1st row: Join thread at top corner of first petal, ch 9, make enough s c in every loop across so that work lies flat. Ch 3, turn. **2nd row:** * Skip 4 s c, 3 d c in next s c, ch 2, 3 d c in same s c, and repeat from * to end of row. Make a chain button-loop at one end at neck and sew button on other end to correspond.

Hostess's Delight

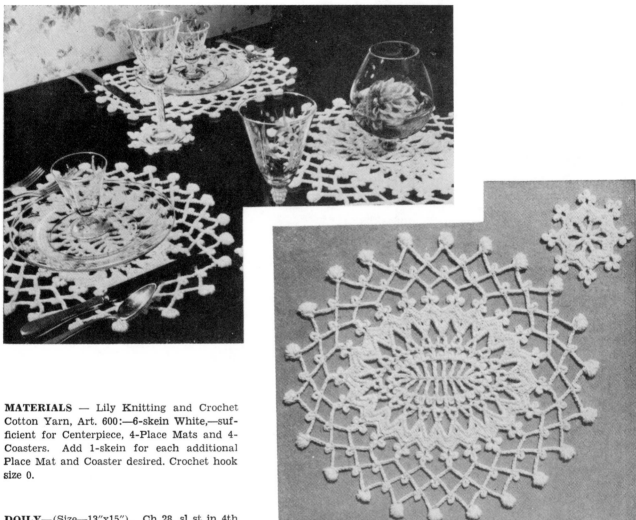

MATERIALS — Lily Knitting and Crochet Cotton Yarn, Art. 600:—6-skein White,—sufficient for Centerpiece, 4-Place Mats and 4-Coasters. Add 1-skein for each additional Place Mat and Coaster desired. Crochet hook size 0.

DOILY—(Size—13"x15"). Ch 28, sl st in 4th st from hook for a p, ch 1, sk p, tr in next 6th st, (ch 4, p, ch 1, tr in next 2d ch st) 9 times to end, ch 4, p, ch 1, tr in same end st, (ch 4, p, ch 1, tr in next 2d st on other side of ch) 8 times, ch 4, p, ch 1, sl st in 1st ch st before first p. **ROW** 2—Ch 9, hdc in 6th ch st from hook, turn, dc in next tr, * (ch 6, hdc in 6th ch st from hook, dc in next tr) * 8 times, (ch 6, hdc in 6th ch st from hook) twice, dc in next tr. Repeat from * to * 9 times. (Ch 6, hdc in 6th ch st from hook) twice, sl st in 3d st of 1st ch. **ROW** 3—Sl st to center of next lp, (ch 9, sc in next lp) repeated around. **ROW** 4—Ch 1, turn, (4 sc, 3 sc in center st, and 4 sc) in each lp. Sl st in 1st sc. **ROW** 5—Ch 1, turn, sk sl st and last 2 sc, and working in back lp of each st, * sc in next 3 sc, 3 sc in next (center) sc, sc in next sc, sk 4 sc in angle and repeat from * around. Sl st in 1st sc. **ROW** 6—Ch 1, turn, sk sl st and last sc, and working in back lps, * sc in next 4 sc, (ch 4, sl st in 4th ch st from hook for a p) 3 times, ch 1, sc in same st on point, sc in next 3 sc, sk 2 sc in angle and repeat from * around and join. Fasten off. **ROW** 7—Join to center p on one point, (ch 9, sc in next point) 21 times, ch 4, tr in next point. **ROW** 8—(Ch 9, sc in 5th st of next lp, going under 2 lps of st, ch 4, sc in same st) repeated around. Fasten off. **ROW** 9—Join to 5th st of one lp, * ch 10, (yarn over, swing hook forward and down, yarn over under ch,

swing hook forward and up again) 7 times over the last 4 ch sts (a Clones Knot) working loosely. Yarn over and pull thru all 15 lps on hook at once, yarn over and thru single lp on hook, pulling it down very tightly, sl st in ch st at base of Knot (the 6th st of 10-ch), ch 5, (sc, ch 4, sc) in 5th st of next lp. Repeat from * around. Fasten off. Make 5 for Centerpiece and 4 Place Mats.

COASTER—Ch 6, sl st in 1st st. Ch 8, dc in ring, (ch 5, dc in ring) 6 times, ch 5, sl st in 3d st of 1st ch. **ROW** 2—Ch 1, turn, (2 sc, 3 sc in center st, and 2 sc) in each lp. Sl st in 1st sc. **ROW** 3—Ch 1, turn, sk last sc and working in back lps, * sc in next 3 sc, (ch 4, sl st in 4th ch st from hook for a p) 3 times, ch 1, sc in same st on point, sc in next 2 sc, sk 2 sc in angle and repeat from * around, join and fasten off. Make 4. Stretch and pin right-side-down. Steam and press dry thru a cloth.

Emerald Isle Tablecloth

MATERIALS: J. & P. Coats or Clark's O.N.T. Best Six Cord Mercerized Crochet, *Size 30:* **Small Ball:** J. & P. Coats—*82 balls of White or Ecru, or 100 balls of any color, or* Clark's O.N.T.—*123 balls of White or Ecru, or 142 balls of any color.* **Big Ball:** J. & P. Coats—*51 balls of White or Ecru, or 64 balls of any color . . . Steel Crochet Hook No. 10.*

GAUGE: Each motif measures 2⅞ inches square.

FIRST MOTIF . . . Starting at center, ch 10. Join with sl st to form ring. **1st rnd:** 20 sc in ring. Sl st in first sc. **2nd rnd:** Ch 1, sc in same place as sl st, sc in next 4 sc, * ch 8, turn; skip 4 sc, sl st in next sc, turn; 15 sc in loop, sc in next 5 sc. Repeat from * around, ending with sl st in first sc made. **3rd rnd:** * Ch 9, sc in center sc at top of next loop, ch 9, sc between loops. Repeat from * around. Join. **4th rnd:** 11 sc in each loop around. Sl st in first sc. **5th rnd:** Ch 8, * sc in center sc of same loop, ch 5, in first sc of next loop make dc, ch 5 and dc; ch 5. Repeat from * around, ending with dc, ch 5, sl st in 3rd ch of ch-8. **6th rnd:** Sl st in next 2 ch, in same loop make sc, ch 3 and sc; * ch 6, in next loop make sc, ch 3 and sc; ch 6, holding back on hook the last loop of each tr make 3 tr in next loop, thread over and draw through all loops on hook (cluster made); ch 3, cluster in same loop, (ch 6, in next loop make sc, ch 3 and sc) twice; ch 6, skip next loop, in next loop make sc, ch 3 and sc. Repeat from * around, ending with ch 2, tr in first sc. **7th rnd:** In loop made by ch 2 and tr make sc, ch 3 and sc; (ch 6, in next ch-6 loop make sc, ch 3 and sc) twice; * ch 6, in sp between clusters make cluster, ch 3 and cluster; (ch 6, in next ch-6 loop make sc, ch 3 and sc) 5 times. Repeat from * around. Join as for previous rnd. **8th rnd:** In loop just formed make *(Continued on page 46)*

(Continued on page 46)

Irish Mist Centerpiece

**Materials Required—AMERICAN THREAD COMPANY
"STAR" or "GEM" MERCERIZED CROCHET
COTTON, Size 20 or 30**

3—300 Yd. Balls White, Ecru, Dark Cream or Colors.
Steel Crochet Hook No. 11 or 12.
Each Motif measures about 4½ inches.
Doily measures about 22 inches through the center.

Motif. 1st Row. * Ch 4, sl st in 4th st from hook for picot, repeat from * 5 times, join.

2nd Row. Ch 3, dc in same space, * ch 4, sl st in 4th st from hook for picot, repeat from *, ch 1, 2 d c between next 2 picots, * double picot loop, ch 1, 2 d c between next 2 picots, repeat from * all around, join.

3rd Row. Ch 3, 2 d c in next d c, * 3 picot loop, ch 1, 1 d c in next d c, 2 d c in next d c, repeat from * all around, join.

4th row. Ch 3, 2 d c in next d c, 1 d c in next d c, * 4 picot loop, ch 1, 1 d c in next d c, 2 d c in next d c, 1 d c in next d c, repeat from * all around, join.

5th Row. Ch 3, 1 d c in next d c, 2 d c in next d c, 1 d c in next d c, * ch 11, 1 d c in each of the next 2 d c, 2 d c in next d c, 1 d c in next d c, repeat from * all around, join.

6th Row. Ch 1, 1 s c in each d c, * 6 s c over loop, ch 4, sl st in top of last s c for picot, 3 s c over same loop, ch 9, turn, sl st in 3rd s c on left side of picot, ch 3, turn, 8 d c over loop just made, ch 4, sl st in top of last dc for picot, 3 d c over same loop, ch 10, turn, sl st in 3rd d c on left side of picot, ch 3, turn, * 9 d c over loop just made, picot, 4 d c over same loop, ch 12, turn, sl st in 4th d c on left side of picot, ch 3, turn, 10 d c over loop just made, picot, 10 d c over same loop, ch 3, sl st in same loop, 5 d c over remainder of next loop, ch 3, sl st in same loop, 5 d c over remainder of next loop, ch 3, sl st in same loop, 3 s c over remainder of ch 11 in previous row, ** 1 s c in each d c, repeat between *, 1 d c over loop just made, ch 7, sl st in 4th st from hook for picot, ch 3, turn, d tr c in center s c between scallops, ch 7, picot, ch 3, sl st in top corner of 2nd scallop, ch 5, turn, sl st in 4th st from hook for picot, ch 5, sl st in 4th st from hook for picot, ch 1, d tr c in d tr c, ch 5, sl st in 4th st from hook for picot, ch 7, sl st in 4th st from hook for picot, ch 1, d tr c in same space, ch 5, picot, ch 5, picot, ch 1, sl st in top of d c over ch 12, 8 d c over same loop, picot, 4 d c over same loop, ch 15, turn, sl st in 4th d c on left side of picot, ch 3, turn, 5 d c over loop just made, ch 6, turn, d tr c in next d tr c, ch 6, d tr c between next 2 picots, ch 6, d tr c in same space, ch 6, d tr c in next d tr c, ch 6, sl st in 5th d c of scallop,

(Continued on page 46)

Bouquet

ROYAL SOCIETY SIX CORD CORDICHET, Large Ball,
Size 30, 2 balls of (No. 3012) Lt. Steel Blue, 1 ball each of (No. 3011) Blue and (No. 3020) Nile Green.

ROYAL SOCIETY TATTING COTTON, 9 balls of White.

Steel Crochet Hooks No. 10 and No. 14.

Doily measures 18 inches in diameter.

Starting at Center with Lt. Steel Blue and No. 10 hook, ch 20. Join with sl st to form ring. **1st rnd:** Ch 4, * dc in next ch, ch 1. Repeat from * around. Join to 3rd ch of ch-4. **2nd rnd:** In each sp around make sc, half dc and sc. Join. **3rd rnd:** Sl st around bar of starting chain in first rnd, ch 4, * dc around bar of next dc, ch 1. Repeat from * around. Join to 3rd ch of ch-4. **4th rnd:** In each sp around make sc, 3 half dc and sc. Join. **5th rnd:** Sl st around bar of starting chain on last dc rnd, ch 5, * dc around bar of next dc, ch 2. Repeat from * around. Join. **6th and 7th rnds:** Repeat 4th and 5th rnds. **8th rnd:** In each sp around make sc, 3 half dc and sc. Join. **9th rnd:** Repeat 5th rnd. **10th rnd:** In each sp around make sc, 4 dc and sc. Join. **11th rnd:** Repeat 5th rnd starting with ch 6 and having ch-3 sps around. Join. **12th and 13th rnds:** Repeat 10th and 11th rnds. **14th rnd:** In each sp around make sc, 5 dc and sc. Join. **15th rnd:** Repeat 11th rnd. **16th rnd:** Repeat 14th rnd. **17th rnd:** Repeat 11th rnd, starting with ch 7 and making ch-4

sps around. Join. **18th rnd:** In each sp around make sc, 6 dc and sc. Join. **19th rnd:** Repeat 17th rnd. **20th rnd:** In each sp around make sc, 7 dc and sc. Join. **21st rnd:** Repeat 11th rnd, starting with ch 8 and having ch 5 sps around. Join. **22nd rnd:** In each sp around make sc, 8 dc and sc. Join. **23rd rnd:** Repeat 21st rnd. **24th rnd:** In each sp around make sc, 9 dc and sc. Join. **25th rnd:** Repeat 11th rnd, starting with ch 9 and having ch 6 sps. Join. **26th rnd:** In each sp around make sc, 2 dc, 6 tr, 2 dc and sc. Join. **27th rnd:** Repeat 25th rnd. **28th rnd:** In each sp around make sc, 2 dc, 7 tr, 2 dc and sc. Join and break off. **29th rnd:** Attach Green to first sc on any scallop, sc in same place, * ch 3, skip 2 sts, sc in next st, ch 2, skip 2 sts, in next st make sc, ch 3, sc, ch 5, sc, ch 3 and sc; ch 3, skip 2 sts, sc in next st, ch 3, sc in first sc on next scallop. Repeat from * around. Join and break off.

FIRST RND OF FLOWERS — First Flower . . . Starting at center with Lt. Steel Blue, ch 10. Join with sl st to form

ring. **1st to 5th rnds incl:** Repeat 1st to 5th rnds incl of Center. **6th rnd:** Repeat 10th rnd. Break off. **7th rnd:** Attach Green to first sc of any scallop, ch 2, skip 2 dc, in next dc make sc, ch 3 and sc; ch 2, sc in first sc of next scallop, ch 2, skip 2 dc, sc in next dc, ch 3, sl st in any ch-5 loop on Center, ch 3, sc in same dc on Flower, * ch 2, sc in first sc on next petal, ch 2, skip 2 dc, in next dc make sc, ch 3 and sc. Repeat from * around. Join and break off.

SECOND FLOWER . . . Work as for First Flower until 6 rnds are completed. **7th rnd:** Attach Green to first sc of any scallop, sc in same place, ch 2, skip 2 dc, sc in next dc, ch 3, sl st in 3rd loop to the right of joining on First Flower, ch 1, sc in same dc on Second Flower, ch 2, sc in first sc on next petal, ch 2, skip 2 dc, sc in next dc, ch 1, sl st in corresponding loop on First Flower, ch 1, sc in same dc on Second Flower, ch 2, sc in first sc on next petal, ch 2, skip 2 dc, sc in next dc, ch 3, sl st in next

(Continued on page 46)

Rose Wreath

Doily measures 14 inches in diameter.

COATS & CLARK'S O.N.T. TATTING-CROCHET, Art. C.21, Size 70: 6 balls of No. 1 White.

Milwards Steel Crochet Hook No. 14.

Starting at center, ch 10. Join with sl st to form ring. **1st rnd:** Cut 16 strands of thread, each 10 inches long. Working over these strands, make 20 sc in ring. Join with sl st to first sc. Cut off remaining strands. **2nd rnd:** Ch 4, * dc in next sc, ch 1. Repeat from * around. Join to 3rd ch of ch-4. **3rd rnd:** Cut 16 strands of thread, each 10 inches long. Working over these strands, make sc in same place as sl st, * 2 sc in next sp, sc in next dc. Repeat from * around. Join. Cut off remaining strands. **4th rnd:** Sc in same place as sl st, * ch 5, skip 2 sc, sc in next sc. Repeat from * around. Join. **5th and 6th rnds:** Sl st to center of next loop, sc in same loop, * ch 5, sc in next loop. Repeat from * around. Join. Break off at end of 6th rnd. **7th rnd:** Ch 15, drop loop from hook, insert hook in any loop on last rnd, draw dropped loop through, * make 5 sc, ch 3 and 5 sc over bar of ch-15, ch 15, drop loop from hook and, working from left to right, insert hook in next loop preceding last loop worked, draw dropped loop through. Repeat from * around, ending with 5 sc, ch 3 and 5 sc over last ch-15 bar, drop loop from hook, insert hook in first loop of starting chain, draw dropped loop through, thus joining rnd. **8th rnd:** 9 sc in first sp, * 5 sc in next sp, ch 12, drop loop from hook, insert hook in center sc of 9-sc group, draw dropped loop through, make 12 sc in loop just formed, ch 8, drop loop from hook, insert hook in 6th sc of 12-sc group, draw dropped

loop through, in loop just formed make 5 sc, ch 3 and 5 sc; 5 sc in next incompleted loop, 4 sc in next incompleted sp, 9 sc in next sp. Repeat from * around. Join and break off.

9th rnd: Attach thread to ch-3 loop on any point, sc in same loop, * ch 10, holding back on hook the last loop of each tr tr, make tr tr at base of same point and at base of next point, thread over and draw through all loops on hook (joint tr tr made), ch 10, sc in next ch-3 loop. Repeat from * around. Join. **10th rnd:** Cut 16 strands of thread, each 25 inches long. Working over these strands, make 12 sc in each sp around. Join. Cut off remaining strands. **11th rnd:** Sc in same place as sl st, * ch 6, skip 3 sc, sc in next sc. Repeat from * around. Join (60 loops). **12th to 15th rnds incl:** Sl st to center of next loop, sc in same loop, * ch 6, sc in next loop. Repeat from * around. Join. Break off at end of 15th rnd. **16th and 17th rnds:** Repeat 7th and 8th rnds. **18th rnd:** Attach thread to ch-3 loop on any point, sc in same place, * ch 12, sc in next loop. Repeat from * around. Join. **19th rnd:** Cut 16 strands of thread, each 1¼ yards long. Working over these strands, make 15 sc in each sp around. Join. Cut off remaining strands. **20th rnd:** Sc in same place as sl st, * ch 7, skip 4 sc, sc in next sc. Repeat from * around. Join (90 loops). **21st to 24th rnds incl:** Repeat 12th to 15th rnds incl, making ch-7 loops (instead of ch-6). **25th and 26th rnds:** Repeat 7th and 8th rnds. **27th rnd:** Repeat 18th rnd. **28th rnd:** Cut 16 strands of thread, each 1½ yards long. Working over these strands, make 16 sc in each sp around. Join and break off. Cut off remaining strands.

(Continued on page 45)

25

Galway Bay Bedspread

If you're an artist with a crochet hook, create this
confection of Irish crochet . . . flower fragility set in smart squares.

MATERIALS:

SINGLE SIZE

J. & P. COATS KNIT-CRO-SHEEN, 60 balls of White
or Ecru, or 72 balls of any color.

OR

CLARK'S O.N.T. LUSTERSHEEN, 45 skeins of White
or Ecru, or 60 skeins of any color.

DOUBLE SIZE

J. & P. COATS KNIT-CRO-SHEEN, 75 balls of White
or Ecru, or 90 balls of any color.

OR

CLARK'S O.N.T. LUSTERSHEEN, 57 skeins of White
or Ecru, or 75 skeins of any color.

MILWARD'S STEEL CROCHET HOOK No. 7.

GAUGE:

Each block measures about 5¾ inches square before blocking. For a single size
spread, about 72 x 108 inches, make 12 x 18 blocks. For a double size spread, about
90 x 108 inches, make 15 x 18 blocks.

BLOCK . . . Starting at center, ch 8, join with sl st.
1st rnd: Ch 5, * d c in ring, ch 2. Repeat from * 6
more times, sl st in 3rd st of ch-5 (8 sps). **2nd rnd:**
In each sp make s c, half d c, 2 d c, half d c and s c
(8 petals). **3rd rnd:** * Ch 4, s c in next d c of 1st rnd
(between petals). Repeat from * around, ending with
ch 4, s c in 3rd st of ch-5 below. **4th rnd:** In each loop
make s c, half d c, 3 d c, half d c and s c. **5th rnd:**
* Ch 5, s c in back loop of s c of 3rd rnd (between
petals). Repeat from * around. **6th rnd:** Same as 4th
rnd, making 4 d c instead of 3 d c. **7th rnd:** * Ch 6,
s c in back loop of s c (between petals) on 5th rnd.
Repeat from * around. **8th rnd:** In each loop make
s c, half d c, 2 d c, 2 tr, 2 d c, half d c and s c. **9th rnd:**
Sl st in each st to 1st tr incl., s c between this and
next tr. (Ch 10, s c between tr's of next petal) 7
times; ch 7, d c in 1st s c made.

10th rnd: 4 s c under d c-bar, make 12 s c in each
ch-10 loop, 8 s c in ch-7 loop (96 s c). **11th, 12th
and 13th rnds:** S c in each s c around, joining
13th rnd with sl st to 1st s c of rnd. **14th rnd:** Ch 1,
s c in sl st, s c in next 3 s c; * ch 9, skip 4 s c, s c in
next 20 s c. Repeat from * around, ending with s c in
last 16 s c; join. **15th rnd:** * Ch 5, in next loop make
s c, ch 2, 7 d c, ch 2 and s c. Ch 5, skip 3 s c, s c in next
14 sts. Repeat from * 3 more times. **16th rnd:** * In
next loop make s c, ch 2, 7 d c, ch 2 and s c. Ch 5, skip
next d c-group. In next loop make s c, ch 2, 7 d c, ch 2
and s c; ch 5, skip 2 s c, s c in next 10 s c, ch 5.
Repeat from * 3 more times. Sl st in 1st s c made.
17th rnd: * (Ch 5, skip next d c-group; in next loop
make s c, ch 2, 7 d c, ch 2 and s c) twice. Ch 5, skip
2 s c, s c in next 6 s c; ch 5, in next loop make s c,
ch 2, 7 d c, ch 2 and s c. Repeat from * 3 more times.

18th rnd: * In next loop make s c, ch 2, 7 d c, ch 2
and s c. Ch 7, skip d c-group, in next loop make s c, ch 2,
7 d c, ch 2 and s c. Ch 5, skip d c-group, in next loop
make s c, ch 2, 7 d c, ch 2 and s c. Ch 3, skip 2 s c, s c in
next 2 s c, ch 3, in next loop make s c, ch 2, 7 d c, ch 2
and s c, ch 5. Repeat from * 3 more times. Join to 1st
s c made and fasten off. **19th rnd:** Attach thread to
1st of any 2 adjacent ch-3 loops of last rnd, * ch 3,
s c in next loop; (ch 6, skip d c-group, s c in next
loop) twice. In same loop as last s c make half d c,
3 d c, 4 tr, 3 d c, half d c and s c. (Ch 6, skip d c-group,
s c in next loop) twice. Repeat from * around; join.

20th rnd: Sl st in 1st ch of ch-3, ch 4, tr in next 2
ch, * ch 3, skip 2 ch of next loop, tr in next 3 ch, ch 3,
skip 1 ch of same loop, skip the next s c and 1 ch of
next loop; make d tr in next 3 ch, ch 3. At base of next
petal, between 2nd and 3rd tr, inserting hook from
back of petal, make tr tr, ch 3, tr tr, ch 5, tr tr, ch 3 and
tr tr. Ch 3, skip 2 ch of next loop, d tr in next 3 ch,
ch 3, skip 1 ch of same loop, skip the next s c and 1 st
of next loop; make tr in next 3 ch, ch 3, tr in each ch
of ch-3 loop. Repeat from * around, ending with ch 3,
sl st in 4th ch of ch-4. **21st rnd:** Ch 3, d c in next 2
sts, * 3 d c in next sp, d c in next 3 sts. Repeat from *
to within 1st tr tr of corner, d c in tr tr, 3 d c in next
sp, d c in next tr tr, 2 d c in corner ch-5 sp, 3 d c in
3rd ch of same ch-5, 2 d c in same sp, d c in next st,
3 d c in next sp, and continue thus around, making
3 d c in each ch-3 sp and d c in each st, and working
in each corner ch-5 sp as before; sl st in 3rd st of ch-3.
Fasten off. This completes one block.

Make necessary number of blocks and sew them
together on wrong side with neat over-and-over
stitches. Block to measurements given.

Pretty Edgings for Your Linens

Use J. & P. Coats or Clark's O.N.T. Best Six Cord Mercerized Crochet, Size 30, with
Steel Crochet Hook No. 10 ○ Size 50 (White only) with Steel Crochet Hook No. 12

8013 **1st row:** Ch 6, dc in 6th ch from hook, * ch 6, without turning make dc in top of last dc. Repeat from * for length desired, having an odd number of loops. Ch 9, turn. **2nd row:** Sc in 1st loop, * ch 5, sc in next loop. Repeat from * across. Ch 6, turn. **3rd row:** Sc in 1st loop, ch 13, sc in 2nd ch from hook, then, working over chain to cover it, make 4 sc, * (ch 4, sc in 4th ch from hook —picot made—5 sc over chain) twice; ch 2, sc in next loop, ch 3, sc in next loop, ch 12, turn, sl st between p's on last covered chain, ch 1, turn, 5 sc over chain. Repeat from * across.

9051 EDGING . . . Ch 10. Join to form ring, ch 3, 9 dc in ring, * ch 10, sl st in last dc made, ch 2, sl st in ring where last dc was made, turn, 9 dc in last ring made. Repeat from * across for desired length. Do not break off.

HEADING . . . Ch 10, * 3 dc in ring, ch 5, sc in center dc of next dc-group, ch 5. Repeat from * across, ending with ch 5, sc in center st of last dc-group. Break off.

SCALLOPS . . . **1st row:** Attach thread to end ring, * ch 5, 7 tr in ring, ch 5, sc in center st of next dc-group. Repeat from * across. Ch 1, turn. **2nd row:** ** 3 sc in next loop, ch 5, holding back on hook the last loop of each tr, make tr in next 3 tr, thread over and draw through all loops on hook (cluster made), * ch 5, make another 3-tr cluster having 1st tr in same place as last tr of last cluster. Repeat from * once more, ch 5, 3 sc in next loop. Repeat from ** across. Break off.

INSERTION . . . Same as Edging until Heading is completed. Work along other long side as for Heading.

9052 EDGING . . . **1st row:** * Ch 5, holding back on hook the last loop of each tr make 3 tr in 5th ch from hook, thread over and draw through all loops on hook (cluster made). Repeat from * for desired length (number of clusters should be a multiple of 6). **2nd row:** * Ch 7, make a 4-tr cluster between next 2 clusters, ch 7, sc between next 2 clusters. Repeat from * across. Break off. **3rd row:** Attach thread in cluster preceding first ch-7 loop, in each of next 5 ch-7 loops make 4 sc, p and 4 sc—*to make a p, ch 3 and sc in 3rd ch from hook*—* ch 12, turn, sc between end sc's of 2nd and 3rd loops from hook (directly over cluster below), ch 12, skip the sc's on the following 2 loops, sc directly over next cluster, ch 1, turn. In next ch-12 loop make 4 sc, p, 7 sc, p and 4 sc; 4 sc in next loop, p, 3 sc in same loop, ch 15, turn, sc in center sc on next loop, ch 1, turn. In loop make (4 sc, p) 3 times and 4 sc; in next incompleted loop make 3 sc, p and 4 sc; in each of next 6 ch-7 loops make 4 sc, p and 4 sc. Repeat from * across. Break off.

HEADING . . . Attach thread to end cluster, ch 10, make a 4-tr cluster between next 2 clusters, * ch 10, skip 2 clusters, cluster between 2nd cluster skipped and following cluster. Repeat from * across. Break off.

INSERTION . . . **1st and 2nd rows:** Same as 1st and 2nd rows of Edging. Do not break off. **3rd row:** Ch 8, * sc in next loop, ch 3, sc in next loop, ch 5. Repeat from * across, ending with ch 3, sc in last loop, ch 8, sc in same loop, sc in next loop, ch 8 and work along opposite edge to correspond. Break off.

8337 EDGING — FIRST MOTIF . . . Starting at center, ch 6. Join with sl st to form ring. **1st rnd:** Ch 1, 12 sc in ring, sl st in 1st sc. **2nd rnd:** Ch 1, sc in same place as sl st, * ch 5, skip next sc, sc in next sc. Repeat from * around, joining last ch-5 with sl st in 1st sc. **3rd rnd:** In each loop make sc, half dc, 3 dc, half dc and sc. Join. **4th rnd:** Ch 1, sc in same place as sl st, * ch 5, sc between next 2 sc. Repeat from * around. Join. **5th rnd:** In each loop make sc, half dc, 5 dc, half dc and sc. Join. **6th rnd:** Ch 1, sc in same place as sl st, * (ch 5, sc in 3rd ch from hook) twice; ch 2 (p-loop made), sc between next 2 sc. Repeat from * around. Join. **7th rnd:** Ch 1, sc in same place as sl st, * make a p-loop, sc between p's of next p-loop, make a p-loop, sc in next sc between petals, (ch 5, sc between p's of next loop, ch 5, sc in next sc between petals) twice. Repeat from * once more. Join and break off.

SECOND MOTIF . . . Work same as First Motif until 6th rnd is completed. **7th rnd:** Ch 5, sc in 3rd ch from hook, ch 1, sc between p's of corresponding p-loop on First Motif, ch 4, sc in 3rd ch from hook, p-loop, sc between p's of next p-loop on Second Motif, ch 5, sc in 3rd ch from hook, ch 1, sc between p's of next p-loop on First Motif, ch 4, sc in 3rd ch from hook, ch 2, sc in sc between petals on Second Motif, ch 5, sc between p's of next p-loop on Second Motif and complete rnd as on First Motif. Break off. Make necessary number of motifs, joining them as Second Motif was joined to First Motif.

HEADING . . . Attach thread after 2nd p of 2nd p-loop at end of piece and work along one long edge as follows: **1st row:** Ch 10, dc in next ch-5 loop, * (ch 3, sc in next loop) twice; ch 3, dc in next loop, ch 6, d tr before 1st p of next p-loop, d tr after p of next p-loop on next motif, ch 6, dc in next ch-5 loop. Repeat from * across, ending with d tr before 1st p of p-loop on last motif. Ch 5, sc in 3rd ch from hook. Ch 2, turn. **2nd row:** Sc in ch-6 loop, * ch 5, sc in 3rd ch from hook, ch 2, sc in dc, (ch 5, sc in 3rd ch from hook, ch 2, sc in next sc) twice; ch 5, sc in 3rd ch from hook, ch 2, sc in next dc, (ch 5, sc in 3rd ch from hook, ch 2, sc in next ch-6 loop) twice. Repeat from * across. Break off.

INSERTION . . . Work same as Edging, making Heading along both long edges (see illustration).

9054 EDGING . . . Ch 15, tr in 15th ch from hook, ch 3, turn, 27 dc in loop, * ch 5, turn, sc in 4th dc from hook, (ch 5, skip 2 dc, sc in next st) 8 times; ch 15, turn, skip 1 ch-5 loop, tr in next loop, ch 3, turn, 27 dc in loop, sl st in next tr (at base of turning ch-3). Repeat from * for desired length, ending with 9 ch-5 loops.

HEADING . . . **1st row:** Attach thread to 2nd ch-5 loop, ch 7, * tr in next loop, ch 2, dc in next loop, ch 2, sc in next loop, ch 2, dc in next loop, ch 2, tr in next loop, ch 2, d tr in next loop, ch 2, d tr in 2nd ch-5 loop on next scallop (where tr was made), ch 2. Repeat from * across, ending with d tr. Ch 5, turn. **2nd row:** * Skip the ch-2, dc in next st, ch 2. Repeat from * across. Break off.

SCALLOPS . . . **1st row:** Attach thread to 3rd ch-5 loop, ch 4, 4 tr in same loop, * (ch 3, 5 tr in next loop) 3 times; skip 2 loops on next scallop, 5 tr in next loop. Repeat from * across. Ch 4, turn. **2nd row:** Holding back on hook the last loop of each tr make tr in next 4 tr, thread over and draw through all loops on hook (cluster made); * (ch 7, make a 5-tr cluster over next 5 tr) twice; ch 7, holding back on hook the last loop of each tr make tr in next 3 tr, skip 4 tr, tr in next 3 tr, thread over and draw through all loops on hook. Repeat from * across. Ch 1, turn. **3rd row:** In each ch-7 loop make (3 sc, ch 3) 4 times and 3 sc. Break off.

INSERTION . . . Work as for Edging until Heading is completed. Work 2 rows along opposite long side to correspond with Heading. Break off.

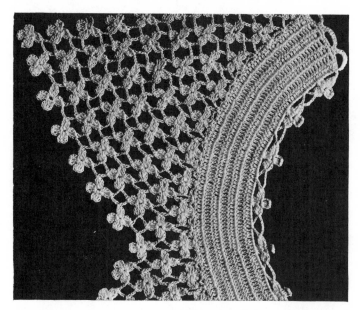

Clover Stitch Collar and Cuffs

Materials: Clark's O.N.T. (4 balls) or J. & P. Coats (3 balls) Mercerized Crochet, size 60, White. Milward's steel crochet hook No. 12. 3 small buttons. 2 snap fasteners.

Collar. The collar is made up of a foundation band of d c's, over which are worked 5 points in clovers (one large point for front, and two small points on each side). Collar is fastened at back with buttons. Cuff is made up in same way as collar, having only 1 point.

Band. Starting at neck, ch 295 (to measure about 20 inches), turn. **1st row:** D c in 4th ch from hook and d c in each ch across (293 d c), ch 3, turn. **2nd to 7th rows incl:** D c in each d c, making 20 increases in each row at regular intervals but do not make an increase over an increase of previous row. (To increase, make 2 d c in 1 d c.) 413 d c in the 7th row.

First Small Point in Clover Pattern. 1st row: Ch 4, skip 2 d c, sl st in the next d c, ch 3, 1 d c in same st as sl st, working off the last 2 loops of d c very loosely, ch 3, 2 d c in loose st (this loose st will be called the center of clover), ch 3, sl st in center, ch 3, 2 d c in center, ch 3, sl st in center, ch 3, 2 d c in center, ch 3, sl st in center, ch 3, 1 d c in center, sl st in first sl st of band (this completes one clover of 4 petals). **2nd row:** Ch 5, skip 3 d c, sl st in next d c of band, ch 3, remove hook, insert it in tip of petal just before last completed petal, and pull loop through, ch 7, 1 d c in 4th ch, making the last 2 sts very loosely (which will be center), ch 3, 2 d c in center, ch 3, sl st in center, ch 3, 2 d c in center, ch 3, sl st in center, ch 3, 2 d c in center, ch 3, sl st in center, ch 3, 1 d c in center, sl st to tip of incomplete petal, ch 7, sl st in same st as sl st of band. **3rd row:** Ch 5, skip 3 d c, sl st in next d c of band, ch 3, 1 d c in same st as sl st, working off last 2 loops very loosely, ch 3, 2 d c in loose st which is center. Remove hook, insert it in 4th ch of ch-7, and pull loop through, ch 3, sl st in center, ch 3, 1 d c in center, ch 3, remove hook, insert it in tip of adjacent free petal of completed clover and pull loop through, ch 7, 1 d c in 4th ch making last 2 sts very loosely which is center, ch 3, 2 d c in center, ch 3, sl st in center, ch 3, 2 d c in center, ch 3, sl st in center,

ch 3, 2 d c in center, ch 3, sl st in center, ch 3, 1 d c in center, sl st to tip of first incomplete petal, * ch 7, sl st to tip of incomplete petal of next clover, 1 d c in center, ch 3, sl st in center, ch 3, 2 d c in center, ch 3, sl st in center, ch 3, 1 d c in center, sl st to tip of other incomplete petal in band. **4th row:** Ch 5, skip 3 d c, sl st in next d c of foundation, ch 3, remove hook, insert it in tip of petal just before last completed petal, and pull loop through, ch 7, 1 d c in 4th ch making the last 2 sts very loosely, which is center, ch 3, 1 d c in center, remove hook, insert it in 4th ch of ch-7, pull loop through, 1 d c in center, ch 3, sl st in center, ch 3, d c in center, ch 3, remove hook, insert it in tip of adjacent free petal of next clover and draw loop through, ch 1, d c in 4th ch working the last 2 loops loosely (center), ch 3, 2 d c in center, ch 3, sl st in center, ch 3, 2 d c in center, ch 3, sl st in center, ch 3, 2 d c in center, ch 3, sl st in center, ch 3, 1 d c in center, sl st to tip of incomplete petal, and thus work back to complete the row as in previous rows. One clover is being increased in every other row. **5th to 10th rows incl:** Continue to work in this way until there are 5 clovers in each of last 2 rows (10 clovers in a line, counting from the first clover made and along outside edge). This completes one half of first small point. **11th row:** Work same as before until the 2nd petal of the 5th clover has been completed, then make 2 more petals on the same clover omitting the connecting chains, then, complete the incompleted petal of same clover, ch 7, sl st to tip of incompleted petal of next clover, and finish row as before. (5 clovers in this row). Thus decrease 1 clover in every other row at the outer edge until there are 2 clovers in each of last 2 rows (8 clovers in a line, counting from the 10th clover and along outside edge).

Begin Second Small Point. Increase 1 clover in every other row (as in first half of first point) until 8 clovers are completed counting from the 8th clover of first point and along outside edge; then decrease as in second half of first point, until 8 clovers (counting along outside edge) are completed.

Now Begin Front Point. Increase 1 clover in every other row until there are 22 clovers in a row counting from the 8th clover of 2nd point and along outside edge. Decrease as before, and work the next

two points in the same way as first two points, and finish off. **Heading.** With right side of collar towards you join thread to foundation ch, at your left. **1st row:** * Ch 7, 2 d c in 4th ch, making the last 2 loops of d c very loosely, which is center, ch 3, 2 d c in center remove hook, insert it in 6th st of foundation ch, pull loop through, ch 3, sl st to center, ch 3, 2 d c in center, ch 3, remove hook, skip 5 ch of foundation, insert hook in next ch, pull loop through and repeat from * to end of row ending row with a clover, ch 3. **2nd row:** * Sl st in center, ch 3, 2 d c in center, ch 3, sl st in center, ch 3, sl st to tip of next petal, ch 3, sl st to petal of next clover,

ch 3, and repeat from * to end of row. Work 1 row of s c down each side of d c band and make 3 chain loops for buttonholes on right side. Sew buttons to correspond on opposite side of collar and finish off.

Cuffs. Band: Ch 66, turn. **1st row:** D c in 4th ch from hook and d c in each ch across (64 d c), ch 3, turn. **2nd and 3rd rows:** D c in each d c, ch 3, turn. **Clover Pattern.** Work as same as for collar for 11 rows (11 clovers in a line counting from the first clover made and along outside edge). Then decrease (as in collar) to correspond. **Heading.** Same as for collar. Fasten cuffs with snaps.

Rose of Erin

Choose your Thread Size—

Using Size 50 thread and No. 12 hook, doily measures 15 inches in diameter

Using Size 30 thread and No. 10 hook, doily measures 18 inches in diameter

Using Size 20 thread and No. 9 hook, doily measures 20 inches in diameter

J. & P. COATS BIG BALL BEST SIX CORD MERCERIZED CROCHET, Art. A.104, Size 50: 2 balls of White; or

CLARK'S BIG BALL MERCERIZED CROCHET, Art. B.34, Size 50: 2 balls of White.

Milwards Steel Crochet Hook No. 12.

Starting at center, ch 9. Join with sl st to form ring. **1st rnd:** 16 sc in ring, sl st in first sc made. **2nd rnd:** Sc in same place as sl st, * ch 5, skip 1 sc, sc in next sc. Repeat from * around, ending with ch 5, sl st in first sc. **3rd rnd:** Sc in same place as sl st, * 2 sc in ch-5 sp, ch 4, sc in next sc. Repeat from * around, ending with sl st in first sc. **4th to 15th rnds incl:** * Sc in next sc and in each remaining sc of sc group, 2 sc in ch-4 sp, ch 4, skip first sc of next sc group. Repeat from * around (15 sc in each sc group on last rnd). Join as before. **16th rnd:** * Sc in next 13 sc, ch 4, sc in ch-4 sp, ch 4, skip next sc. Repeat from * around. Join. **17th rnd:** * Sc in next 11 sc, (ch 5, sc in next

32

loop) twice; ch 5, skip next sc. Repeat from * around. Join. Continue in this manner, having 2 sc less in each sc group and 1 loop more between sc groups on each rnd until 1 sc remains in each sc group, ending with ch 2, dc in first sc. Now work as follows: **1st rnd:** * Ch 2, sc in next loop, (ch 5, sc in next loop) 7 times. Repeat from * around, ending with ch 2, dc in dc. **2nd rnd:** * Ch 5, skip ch-2 loop, sc in next loop, (ch 5, sc in next loop) 6 times. Repeat from * around, ending as previous rnd. **3rd and 4th rnds:** * Ch 5, sc in next loop. Repeat from * around, ending with ch 2, dc in dc. **5th rnd:** Ch 5, sc in next loop, * ch 5, 6 dc in next loop; (ch 5, sc in next loop) 6 times. Repeat from * around. Join as before. **6th rnd:** (Ch 5, sc in next loop) twice; * ch 5, sc between 3rd and 4th dc of dc group, (ch 5, sc in next loop) 7 times. Repeat from * around. Join. **7th rnd:** * Ch 5, sc in next loop. Repeat from * around, increasing 1 loop evenly around—*to inc 1 loop, make (sc, ch 5) twice in same loop.* Join and break off (65 loops).

FIRST ROSETTE . . . Ch 10, join. **1st rnd:** 24 sc in ring; join. **2nd rnd:** * Ch 5, skip 3 sc, sc in next sc. Repeat from * around (6 loops). Join. **3rd rnd:** In each loop around make sc, half dc, 3 dc, half dc and sc; join. **4th rnd:** * Ch 5, sc in back loop of sc between this and next petal. Repeat from * around (6 loops). Join. **5th rnd:** In each loop around make sc, ch 2, 7 dc, ch 2 and sc; join. **6th rnd:** Sl st in each of next 2 ch, sc in same place as last sl st, * ch 5, skip 3 dc, sc in next dc, ch 5, sc in first ch of next ch-2, ch 5, sc in 2nd ch of next ch-2. Repeat from * around. Join to first sc. **7th rnd:** Sl st to center of first loop, sc in same loop, * ch 6, sc in next loop. Repeat from * around. Join. **8th rnd:** Sl st to center of first loop, sc in same loop, ch 7, sc in next loop, * ch 3, sc in center of one loop on last rnd of center, ch 3, sc in next loop on rosette. Repeat from * 5 more times (6 loops joined). Make a ch-7 loop in all remaining loops of Rosette; join. Break off.

SECOND ROSETTE . . . Work as for First Rosette until 7 rnds have been completed. **8th rnd:** Sl st to center of first loop, sc in same loop, then join to First Rosette as follows: Ch 3, sc in 2nd free loop after last joining on First Rosette, ch 3, sc in next loop on Second Rosette, ch 3, sc in next loop on First Rosette, ch 3, sc in next loop on Second Rosette, ch 3, sc in same place as the last joining of First Rosette to center, ch 3, sc in next loop on Second Rosette. Join next 5 loops of Second Rosette to next 5 loops on center in same way as First Rosette was joined. Make a ch-7 loop in all remaining loops of rosette; join (10 free loops).

Make 11 more rosettes, joining them in same way and taking care to join the last rosette on both sides.

Now work in rnds as follows: **1st rnd:** Attach thread to first free loop on any motif, ch 9, * (sc in next loop, ch 6) 6 times; dc in next 2 loops, ch 6. Repeat from * around. Join to 3rd ch of ch-9. **2nd rnd:** Sl st to center of next loop, sc in same loop, * ch 6, sc in next loop. Repeat from * around. Join. **3rd rnd:** Sl st to center of next loop, sc in same loop, ch 6, sc in next loop, * 7 dc in next loop, sc in next loop, (ch 6, sc in next

loop) 4 times. Repeat from * around. Join. **4th rnd:** Sl st to center of next loop, sc in same loop, * ch 6, sc in center dc of next group, (ch 6, sc in next loop) 4 times. Repeat from * around. Join (75 loops). **5th rnd:** Sl st to center of next loop, sc in same loop, * ch 7, sc in next loop. Repeat from * around. Join. **6th rnd:** Inc 5 loops evenly around. Join and break off.

FIRST PINWHEEL MOTIF . . . Work as for center of doily until there are 7 sc on each group. **8th rnd:** Sc in next 5 sc, * ch 5, sc in next sp, ch 5, skip 1 sc, sc in next 5 sc. Repeat from * around. Join. **9th rnd:** Sc in next 3 sc, * (ch 5, sc in next loop) twice; ch 5, skip 1 sc, sc in next 3 sc. Repeat from * around. Join. **10th rnd:** Sc in next sc, * (ch 5, sc in next loop) 3 times; ch 5, skip 1 sc, sc in next sc. Repeat from * around, ending with ch 2, dc in first sc.

To Join Motif to Center: 11th rnd: Ch 3, sl st in any loop on center, ch 3, sc in next loop on motif, (ch 3, sl st in next loop on center, ch 3, sc in next loop on motif) twice; * ch 7, sc in next loop. Repeat from * around. Join.

SECOND PINWHEEL MOTIF . . . Work as for First Pinwheel Motif until 10 rnds have been completed. **11th rnd:** Ch 3, sl st in 6th free loop on First Pinwheel Motif, ch 3, sc in next loop on Second Pinwheel Motif, (ch 3, sl st in next loop on First Pinwheel Motif, ch 3, sc in next loop on Second Pinwheel Motif) twice; (ch 7, sc in next loop) 3 times; skip 2 loops on center, join next 3 loops on motif to center as before. Complete rnd as for First Pinwheel Motif.

Make 14 more motifs, joining to preceding motif and to center as before. Join last motif to first motif.

FILL-IN-MOTIF . . . Attach thread to first free loop on center, ch 4, tr in same loop, holding back on hook the last loop of each tr, make 2 tr in next loop, thread over and draw through all loops on hook (cluster made), make a cluster in each free loop on motif. Join and break off.

Fill in all sps the same way.

EDGING . . . **1st rnd:** Attach thread to 3rd free loop on any motif, sc in same place, * (ch 7, sc in next loop) 12 times; ch 3, dc in next loop, tr in next 2 loops, dc in next loop, ch 3, sc in next loop. Repeat from * around. Join. **2nd rnd:** Sl st to center of next loop, ch 4, tr in next loop, * (ch 7, sc in next loop) 8 times; ch 7, holding back on hook the last loop of each tr make tr in next 4 loops, thread over and draw through all loops on hook (joint cluster made). Repeat from * around, ending with a 2-tr cluster. Join to top of first tr. **3rd rnd:** 5 sc in next loop, * (ch 7, sc in next loop) 7 times; ch 7, 5 sc in each of next 2 loops. Repeat from * around. Join. **4th rnd:** Sc in first 5 sc, * 5 sc in next loop, (ch 10, sc in next loop) 6 times; ch 10, 5 sc in next loop, sc in next 10 sc. Repeat from * around. Join. **5th rnd:** Sc in same place as sl st, * ch 3, in each of next 7 loops make 6 sc, ch 3, sc in 3rd ch from hook (picot made) and 6 sc; ch 3, sc in center of next sc group. Repeat from * around. Join and break off. Starch lightly and press.

County Clare Bedspread

Materials Required — AMERICAN THREAD COMPANY "PURITAN" MERCERIZED CROCHET AND KNITTING COTTON, ARTICLE 40 or "TROJAN" MERCERIZED CROCHET AND KNITTING COTTON, ARTICLE 33

43—300 yd. Balls White, Ecru, Cream or Beige.
Steel Crochet Hook No. 6 or No. 7.

Each Motif measures about 5 inches. 216 Motifs (12 x 18) are required to make spread measuring about 62 x 92 inches without the 7 inch fringe.

Ch 6, join to form a ring.

2nd Row. Ch 7, d c in ring, * ch 3, d c in same ring, repeat from * 5 times, ch 3, join in 4th st of ch.

3rd Row. Ch 1, 2 s c in 1st mesh, ** ch 14, d c in 6th st from hook, * ch 2, skip 2 sts of ch, d c in next st, repeat from * ch 1, turn.

4th Row. 1 s c in d c, 2 s c in mesh, 1 s c in next d c, 2 s c in next mesh, 1 s c in next d c, 1 s c in each of the next 2 sts of ch, 3 s c in next st of ch, 1 s c in each of the next 2 sts of ch, 1 s c in d c, 2 s c in mesh, 1 s c in d c, 2 s c in mesh, 1 s c in last d c, ch 1, turn.

5th Row. 1 s c in each of the next 10 s c, picking up the back loop of st only, 3 s c in next st, 1 s c in each of the next 10 s c, ch 1, turn.

6th Row. 1 s c in each of the next 11 s c picking up the back loop of st only, 3 s c in next st, 1 s c in each of the next 11 s c, ** ch 1, turn.

7th Row. 1 s c in each of the next 12 s c picking up the back loop of st only, 3 s c in next st, 1 s c in each of the next 12 s c. With right side of work toward you, sl loop off hook, fold the petal through the center lengthwise, insert hook in 1st st of 7th row, pick up loop and sl st across lower edge and the 2 remaining chs of stem, flatten out petal again, work 2 s c over remainder of 1st mesh, ch 5, sl st in 1st st for picot, 2 s c in next mesh and repeat between ** of 3rd and 6th rows, ch 1, turn.

8th Row. 1 s c in each of the 1st 3 s c, slip loop off hook, insert hook in back loop of corresponding st of previous petal made and pull through loop to join, 1 s c in each of the next 3 s c, join to corresponding st of previous petal, 1 s c in each of the next 6 s c, 3 s c in next st, 1 s c in each of the next 12 s c, complete petal same as previous petal and continue until there are 8 petals joining the last petal to 1st petal made, break thread.

9th Row. Join thread in point of petal, ch 7, d c in same space, * ch 2, skip 1 st, d c in next st, ch 2, skip 1 st, d c in next st, ch 2, skip 1 st, tr c in next st, skip 1st free st on next petal, tr c in next st, ch 2, skip 1 st, d c in next st, ch 2, skip 1 st, d c in next st, ch 2, skip 1 st, d c in point of petal, ch 3, d c in same space, repeat from * all around, ch 2, join in 4th st of ch.

10th Row. Ch 1, * 3 s c in 1st mesh, 1 s c in d c, 2 s c in next mesh, s c in d c, 2 s c in next mesh, s c in d c, 2 s c in next mesh, skip the 2 tr c, 2 s c in each of the next 3 meshes, 1 s c in each of the 3 d c, repeat from * all around.

11th Row. Ch 5, skip 3 s c, 1 s c in each of the next 7 s c, ch 3, skip 4 s c, 1 s c in each of the next 17 s c, ch 3, skip 4 s c, 1 s c in each of the next 7 s c, repeat from beginning all around.

12th Row. Sl st into loop, ch 6, tr c into loop, * ch 1, tr c into same loop, repeat from * 4 times, ** ch 3, skip 1 s c, 1 s c in each of the next 5 s c, ch 4, skip 1 s c of next group of s c, 1 s c in each of the next 15 s c, ch 4, skip 1 s c of next group of s c, 1 s c in each of the next 5 s c, ch 3, 1 tr c in loop, * ch 1, tr c in same loop, repeat from * 5 times and repeat from ** all around, ch 3, join in 5th st of ch.

13th Row. S c into next loop, * ch 3, s c into next loop, repeat from * 5 times, ** ch 3, skip 1 s c, s c in each of the next 3 s c, ch 3, d c into next loop, ch 3, skip 1 s c, 1 s c in each of the next 13 s c, ch 3, d c over loop, ch 3, skip 1 s c, 1 s c in each of the next 3 s c, * ch 3, s c into next loop, repeat from * 7 times and repeat from ** all around completing the loops at corner.

14th Row. Sl st to next loop, ch 2, s c into next loop, ch 2, s c into next loop, ch 3, s c into same loop (this is the corner) * ch 2, s c into next loop, repeat from * 3 times, * ch 2, d c into next loop, repeat from *, ch 2, skip 2 s c, 1 s c in each of the next 9 s c, * ch 2, d c in next loop, repeat from *, * ch 2, s c into next loop, repeat from * 4 times, ch 3, s c into same loop, * ch 2, s c into next loop, repeat from * 3 times and continue all around.

15th Row. Ch 1, 2 s c in each of the next 2 loops, 5 s c in corner loop, 2 s c in each of the next 4 loops, 3 s c in each of the next 3 loops, skip 1 s c, 1 s c in each of the next 7 s c, and continue all around.

16th Row. Working into back loop of st only work 1 s c in each s c to corner st, 3 s c in corner.

Around entire spread work 1 ch meshes, working a d c into every other st.

Across top edge, join thread in d c, * ch 3, 2 d c in same space, skip one mesh, sl st in next mesh, ch 3, 2 d c in same space, skip 1 d c and mesh, sl st in next d c, repeat from * across top edge.

Fringe. Cut 14 lengths, 14 inches long, double these and knot into mesh. Repeat in every other mesh and knot again as illustrated.

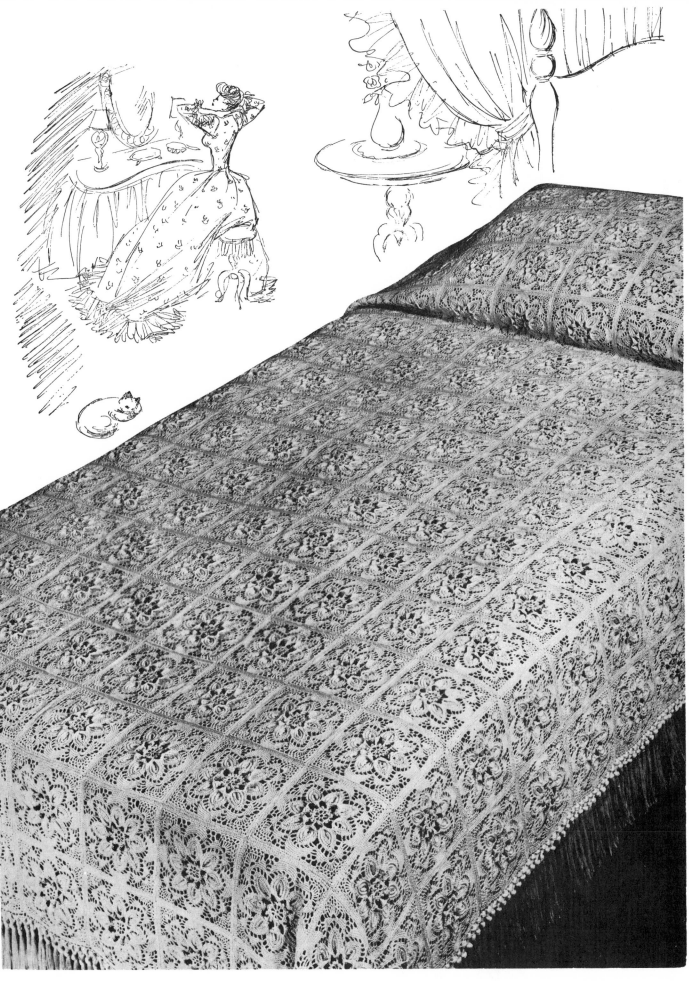

Londonderry Air

Materials

Materials	Quantity	Approx. Size of Motif	Size of Crochet Hook
"DAISY" Mercerized Crochet Cotton Art. 65, Size 20 or 30	1 skein Ecru will make 18 or 25 Motifs	3¾ or 3½ inches across corners	Steel 12 or 13
or			
"DAISY" MERCERIZED CROCHET COTTON Art. 97, Size 20 or 30,	1 ball Ecru will make 11 or 17 Motifs	3¾ or 3½ inches across corners	Steel 12 or 13
or			
"MERCROCHET" COTTON Art. 161, Size 20 or 30	1 ball Ecru will make 11 or 15 Motifs	3¾ or 3½ inches across corners	Steel 12 or 13
or			
"SKYTONE" MERCERIZED CROCHET COTTON Art. 123	1 ball Ecru will make 10 Motifs	5 inches across corners	Steel 10

MOTIF—Starting in center, ch 7, dc in 7th ch from hook, (ch 3, dc in same st) 4 times, ch 3, join with sl st in 3d st of next ch-6; ch 1, sc in same st. Wrap starting end of thread around 1 dc out to edge of circle and work over it in next rnd.

2d rnd—(Ch 1, 5 dc in next sp, ch 1, sc in next dc) repeated around (6 petals), joining with sl st in 1st sc, ch 1, sc in same st.

3d rnd—(Ch 5, sc in back lp of sc between next 2 petals) 5 times, ch 5, join with sl st in 1st sc, ch 1, sc in same st.

4th rnd—(Ch 1, 9 dc in next sp, ch 1, sc in next sc) repeated around, join to 1st sc, sl st to 3d dc on next petal.

5th rnd—Ch 5, sk 3 dc, tr in next dc, * ch 10, tr in same dc and tr in 3d dc on next petal keeping last lp of each tr on hook, thread over and draw thru all 3 lps at one time (2-tr Cluster st), ch 10, (tr in same dc with last tr, sk 3 dc, tr in next dc) made into a Cluster. Repeat from * around, end with ch 10, sl st in 1st tr (12 lps), sl st in next 5 ch sts, sc in same lp.

6th rnd—* (Ch 1, tr) 5 times in next Cluster st, ch 1, sc in next lp, (ch 7, sl st in 1 lp of 5th ch from hook for a p) twice, ch 10, p, ch 7, p, ch 3, sc in next lp. Repeat from * around, join and sl st to center tr of next shell.

7th rnd—Ch 6, tr in same tr, (ch 1, tr) twice in same tr, * ch 10, sl st in last tr for a p, (ch 1, tr) 3 times in same st with last tr, ch 6, p, ch 7, p, ch 2, tr in center st between 2d and 3d ps of next p-lp, ch 6, p, ** ch 10, p, ch 2, tr in same st, ch 6, p, ch 7, p, ch 2, tr in center tr of next shell, (ch 1, tr) 3 times in same tr. Repeat from *

around, join final p-lp to 5th st of 1st ch-6. Cut 6 inches long, thread to a needle and fasten off on back of shell.

2d MOTIF—Repeat to ** in 7th rnd, ch 2, sl st in 1 lp of center ch at tip of 1 point on 1st Motif, ch 7, p, ch 2, tr back in same st with last tr on 2d Motif, ch 6, p, ch 7, p, ch 2, tr in center tr of next shell, (ch 1, tr) 3 times in same st, ch 5, sl st in corresponding p on next shell on 1st Motif, ch 5, sl st back in last tr on 2d Motif, (ch 1, tr) 3 times in same st with last tr, ch 6, p, ch 7, p, ch 2, tr in center st of next p-lp, ch 6, p, ch 2, sl st in 1 lp of center st of next point on 1st Motif, ch 7, p, ch 2, tr back in same st with last tr on 2d Motif and finish rnd as for 1st Motif.

Join Motifs as in Chart, joining adjacent sides as 2d Motif was joined to 1st Motif (where 3 corners meet, join 3d corner to joining of previous 2 corners).

EDGE—Join to p on shell at A on Chart, * ch 15, tr in center ch at tip of next point, (ch 1, tr) 6 times in same st, ch 15, sc in p on next shell, ch 18, dc in joining of Motifs, ch 18, sc in p on next shell, (ch 15, a 7 tr shell in tip of next point with ch-1 between tr, ch 15, sc in p on next shell) twice, ch 18, dc in next joining of Motifs, ch 18, sc in p on next shell. Repeat from * around. Join.

2d rnd—** 4 sc in next lp, ch 5, sl st in last sc for a p, in same lp make (4 sc, a p) twice and 4 sc; (sc in tr, sc in ch-1) repeated to center tr of next shell, a p, (sc in next sp, sc in next tr) 3 times, in next lp make (4 sc, a p) 3 times and 4 sc; in each of next 2 ch-18 lps make 5 sc, a p, (4 sc, a p) twice and 5 sc; * in next ch-15 lp make (4 sc, a p) 3 times and 4 sc; (sc in tr, sc in ch-1) repeated to center tr of next shell, a p, (sc in next sp, sc in next tr) 3 times, in next ch-15 lp make (4 sc, a p) 3 times and 4 sc. Repeat from * once. In each of next 2 ch-18 lps make 5 sc, a p, (4 sc, a p) twice and 5 sc. Repeat from ** around. Join and fasten off.

Stretch and pin doily right-side-down in true shape. Steam and press dry thru a cloth.

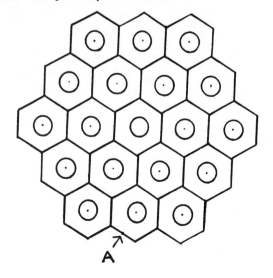

A

ROSE OF SHARON

Rose of Sharon Bedspread

Each motif measures appx. 4½″ square, edge appx. ½″ wide.

Appx. Size	Motifs	Rows
Twin Size 67½″ x 103½″	345	15 wide / 23 long
Double Size 90″ x 103½″	460	20 wide / 23 long

DIRECTIONS

1st Row: Chain 7 and join with a slip stitch to form a ring — ch 2 (for 1st single crochet) — 11 more s c in ring — join to top of ch 2 (total of 12 s c).

2nd Row: Ch 6 — * skip 1 s c — 1 double crochet in next s c — ch 3, repeat from * joining last ch 3 to 3rd st of 1st ch 6 (total of 6 loops).

3rd Row: Over each loop work a petal thus (* 1 s c — 7 d c — 1 s c) — ch 1 between, repeat from * ending with ch 1 and join to 1st s c of 1st petal (total of 6 petals).

4th Row: * Ch 5 — fasten with a sl st over the ch 1 between next two petals at back of work, repeat from * (total of 6 loops).

5th Row: Like 3rd row with (1 s c — 9 d c — 1 s c) over each petal.

6th Row: Like 4th row with ch 6 instead of ch 5.

7th Row: Like 5th row with (1 s c — 11 d c — 1 s c) over each petal.

8th Row: Sl st to 3rd d c of petal —* ch 7 (for a PLAIN LOOP) — skip 5 d c and sl st in 9th d c of petal — ch 7 — sl st in 3rd d c of next petal, repeat from * (total of 12 plain loops)

9th Row: Sl st to center of 1st loop — ** 1 plain loop — sl st to next loop — 1 PICOT LOOP made thus (* ch 6 — fasten back with a sl st in 5th st from hook, repeat from * once more — ch 2) sl st in next loop, this completes a loop with two picots and will hereafter be referred to as a PICOT LOOP — 1 more picot loop — sl st in next loop, repeat from ** 3 more times joining last picot loop to beginning of 1st plain loop (total of 4 plain loops, with 2 picot loops between each).

10th Row: Ch 3 (for 1 d c) — 11 more d c over ch 7 (plain loop) — * 1 picot loop — sl st in next loop between picots — 1 picot loop — sl st in next loop between picots — 1 picot loop — thread over hook and work 12 d c (a shell) over next ch 7, repeat from * ending with picot loop and fasten to top of 1st ch 3 (total of 4 shells, with 3 picot loops between each shell).

11th Row: * Ch 7 — sl st to center of 1st shell — ch 11 — turn work and sl st to ch 7 — ch 1 — turn and work 12 s c over loop fastening with sl st in 4th st of ch (from center of shell) — ch 3 — sl st to last d c of same shell — 4 picot loops fastening last loop in 1st d c of next shell, repeat from * around ending with picot loop fastened to beginning of 1st ch 7 (total of 3 plain loops over each shell, with 4 picot loops between).

12th Row: Sl st up to 1st s c of center loop over shell — ch 3 (for 1 d c) — 1 d c in every s c (making a shell of 12 d c) — * 5 picot loops — 1 d c each in every s c of next shell, repeat from * around ending with 1 picot loop fastened to top of ch 3 of 1st shell (total of 4 shells, with 5 picot loops between).

13th Row: Like 11th row (total of 3 plain loops over each shell, with 6 picot loops between).

14th Row: Like 12th row (total of 4 shells, with 7 picot loops between).

15th Row: 1 picot loop — sl st to center of shell — 1 picot loop — sl st to last d c of shell — * 8 picot loops — 2 picot loops over next shell, repeat from * around ending with 1 picot loop fastened to top of 1st d c of 1st shell of 14th row (total of 40 picot loops, 2 each over each shell with 8 between), fasten off.

This completes the first motif, all of the remaining motifs are made identically the same with the following exception, TO JOIN MOTIFS: when making the last (or 15th) row of picot loops work thus — 1 picot loop — sl st to center of shell — ch 6 — sl st in 5th st from hook — ch 1 — take hook out of work and insert in center of corresponding loop of 1st motif and draw loop through — ch 6 — sl st in 5th st from hook — ch 2 — sl st to center of next picot loop of motif you are now working on. Continue on in this manner until all 10 picot loops on one side of motif have been joined to the corresponding 10 picot loops of the first motif. After completing entire spread work crochet edge as follows.

EDGE

Attach thread in center of a picot loop (between picots) — ch 5 — 1 treble (twice over hook) crochet over the sl st between loops — ch 2 — 1 d c in center of next picot loop — ch 2 — 1 tr between loops — ch 7, take hook out of work and insert in top of 1st tr and draw thread through, then cover loop as follows — 3 s c — ch 5 — 3 s c — ch 5 — 3 s c — ch 5 — 3 s c and sl st in top of tr (this forms a scallop). Work thus all around edge of spread leaving one space of ch 2 between each scallop.

American Beauty

Irish Crochet Roses surrounded by Lacy Leaves

Place Mat measures 15 x 20 inches.

Each Motif measures 3 inches in diameter, including leaves.

J. & P. COATS BIG BALL BEST SIX CORD MERCERIZED CROCHET, Art. A.104, Size 30: 10 balls of No. 65 Beauty Pink and 3 balls of No. 26-B Bright Nile Green.

CLARK'S BIG BALL MERCERIZED CROCHET, Art. B.34, Size 30: 10 balls of No. 65 Beauty Pink and 3 balls of No. 26-B Bright Nile Green.

Milwards Steel Crochet Hook No. 10.

2 yards of pink linen, 36 inches wide.

PLACE MAT (Make 4)—First Motif—Rosette . . . Starting at Center with Beauty Pink, ch 8. Join with sl st to form ring. **1st rnd:** 16 sc in ring. Join to first sc. **2nd rnd:** Sc in same place as sl st, * ch 3, skip 1 sc, sc in next sc. Repeat from * around. Join (8 loops). **3rd rnd:** In each loop around make sc, half dc, 3 dc, half dc, and sc. Join. **4th rnd:** * Ch 3, sc between next 2 petals. Repeat from * around. Join. **5th rnd:** In each loop around make sc, half dc, 5 dc, half dc and sc. **6th to 13th rnds incl:** Repeat 4th and 5th rnds alternately, making 1 ch more on each loop rnd and 1 dc more on each petal rnd (ch-7 loops on 12th rnd, and 9 dc in petals on 13th rnd). Break off at end of 13th rnd.

LEAF . . . **1st row:** With right side of Rosette facing, attach Nile Green to 2nd dc made on any petal, ch 11, turn, sl st in corresponding dc on next petal, turn. **2nd row:** Sc in loop just formed, ch 3, sl st in last sc (picot made); in same loop make (2 sc, picot) 6 times and sc. Sl st in same dc as thread was attached on petal. Break off. Make a leaf between all petals in the same way.

SECOND MOTIF . . . Work as for First Motif until Rosette has been completed.

LEAF . . . With right side of Rosette facing, attach Nile Green to 2nd dc made on any petal, ch 11, turn; sl st in corresponding dc in next petal. Turn. **2nd row:**

Sc in loop just formed, picot, in same loop make (2 sc, picot) twice and 2 sc; ch 1, sl st in center of picot of any leaf on First Motif, ch 1, sc in last sc made on Second Motif, in same loop make (2 sc, picot) 3 times and sc. Complete Leaf as before. Join next Leaf to corresponding Leaf the same way. Complete rnd, no more joinings.

Make 5 motifs for long side, having 2 leaves free on each side of joining. Continuing to keep 2 leaves free on inner edge, join only 1 loop of next 4 motifs to form rounded end. (The 4th motif is the first motif on next long side.) Complete next side and rounded end to correspond. Join Last Motif to First Motif. Place motifs on a piece of linen to form an oval. Baste and sew in place. Cut away excess material and hem raw edges.

APRON—Motif (Make 20) . . . Work exactly as for Motifs of Place Mat. Cut linen 16½ x 27 inches. Curve lower edges. Place Motifs on curved edge and complete as for Place Mat. Gather top edge to measure 15 inches. With remaining material make waistband and ties and sew in place.

Rose of Tralee

Materials Required: AMERICAN THREAD COMPANY
The Famous "PURITAN" Mercerized Crochet Cotton, Article 40
1 ball each White and Nile Green and

The Famous "PURITAN" Star Spangled Mercerized Crochet Cotton, Article 40
1 ball each Pink Spangle and Yellow Spangle
Steel crochet hook No. 7
Approximate size: 10 inches in diameter or
"GEM" MERCERIZED CROCHET COTTON, Article 35, size 30
1 ball each White, Buttercup, Shaded Pinks and Nile Green
Steel crochet hook No. 12
Approximate size: 6½ inches in diameter

ROSE: With Yellow Spangle or Buttercup ch 5, join to form a ring, ch 5, d c in ring, ° ch 2, d c in ring, repeat from ° 3 times, ch 2, join in 3rd st of ch, cut thread. Attach Pink Spangle or Shaded Pinks in loop, 1 s c, 5 d c, 1 s c in same space, ° 1 s c, 5 d c, 1 s c in next loop, repeat from ° 4 times, join.

Next Round. ° Ch 5, sl st in back of work between next 2 petals, repeat from ° 5 times.

Next Round. Over each loop work 1 s c, 7 d c, 1 s c, join.

Next Round. ° Ch 7, sl st in back of work between next 2 petals, repeat from ° all around.

Next Round. Over each loop work 1 s c, 2 d c, 5 tr c, 2 d c, 1 s c, join, cut thread. Work 9 more roses in same manner.

CENTER: With White ch 7, join to form a ring, ch 1 and work 10 s c in ring, join.

2nd Round. Ch 3, 2 d c in same space keeping last loop of each d c on hook, thread over and pull through all loops at one time, ° ch 3, cluster st in next s c (cluster st: 3 d c in same space keeping last loop of each d c on hook, thread over and pull through all loops at one time), repeat from ° 8 times, ch 3, join.

3rd Round. ° Ch 4, s c in next loop, ch 4, s c in next cluster st, repeat from ° all around (20 loops).

4th Round. Sl st into loop, ° ch 4, s c in next loop, repeat from ° all around ending with ch 1, d c in same space as beginning (this brings thread in position for next round).

5th Round. Ch 3 (counts as part of 1st cluster st), cluster st in same space, ° ch 4, s c in next loop, ch 4, cluster st in next loop, repeat from ° all around ending with ch 4, s c in next loop, ch 4, join in 1st cluster st.

6th Round. Sl st into loop, ° ch 5, sc in next loop, repeat from ° all around.

7th Round. Sl st into loop, ch 3, cluster st in same space, ° ch 5, 2 s c in next loop, ch 5, cluster st in next loop, repeat from ° all around ending with ch 5, 2 s c in next loop, ch 5, join.

8th Round. Sl st into loop, ch 1, 2 s c in same space, ° ch 7, 2 s c in next loop, repeat from ° all around ending with ch 3, tr c in 1st s c.

9th Round. Ch 3, cluster st in same space, ch 5, cluster st in same space, ° ch 1, 2 cluster sts with ch 5 between in next loop, repeat from ° all around, ch 1, join, cut thread.

10th Round. Attach Green in the ch 1 between cluster sts, ch 4, cluster st in next ch 5 loop, ch 1, s c in center st of any

(Continued on page 43)

Dainty Irish Crochet Dress

TODDLER SIZES 1 and 2

What You Need

ROYAL SOCIETY SIX CORD CORDICHET

Small Ball, Size 50:
Size 1 — 5 balls.   Size 2 — 6 balls.

Steel Crochet Hook No. 12.

A small pearl button.

GAUGE: Each motif measures about 1½ inches in diameter. 2 picot loops make 1 inch; 4 rows make 1 inch. Directions are written for Toddler size 1; Toddler size 2 appears in parentheses.

Starting at neck edge, ch 151 to measure 11 inches. **1st row:** Sc in 2nd ch from hook and **in next 8 ch**, * 2 sc in next ch (an increase made), sc in next 9 ch. Repeat from * 12 more times; sc in remaining ch (163 sts). Ch 1, turn. **2nd row:** Sc in 1st sc, * ch 6, sc in 4th ch from hook (p made), ch 5, sc in 4th ch from hook, ch 3 (a p loop made), sk 5 sts, sc in next st. Repeat from * across (27 p loops). Fasten off.

First Medallion . . . Starting at center, ch 11, join with sl st to form ring. **1st rnd:** Ch 1, 18 sc in ring. Join with sl st in 1st sc. **2nd rnd:** Ch 1, sc in same place as sl st, * ch 5, sk 2 sts, sc in next st. Repeat from * around, joining last ch-5 with sl st in 1st sc (6 loops). **3rd rnd:** In each loop make sc, h dc, 5 dc, h dc and sc. Join. **4th rnd:** * Ch 6, sc in back of next sc on 2nd rnd. Repeat from * around. Join last ch-6 with sl st in first st of first ch-6 (6 loops). **5th rnd:** * In next loop make sc, h dc, 5 dc, h dc and sc; sc in next sc. Repeat from * around. Join. **6th rnd:** * Make a p loop, sc in center dc of next petal, p loop, sc in sc between

petals. Repeat from * around. Join with sl st in base of 1st p loop. **7th rnd:** Sl st across to between p's of 1st p loop, ch 6, sc in 4th ch from hook, ch 1, sc in end p loop on neckband, ch 5, sc in 4th ch from hook, ch 3, sc in next p loop on medallion, * ch 6, sc in 4th ch from hook, ch 1, sc in next p loop on neckband, ch 5, sc in 4th ch from hook, ch 3, sc in next p loop on medallion. Repeat from * once more (3 joinings), finish remainder of rnd with p loops. Fasten off.

Second Medallion . . . Work as for 1st medallion until 6th rnd is complete. **7th rnd:** Sl st across to between p's of 1st p loop, ch 6, sc in

42

4th ch from hook, ch 1, sc in 2nd p loop (from last joining) on 1st medallion, join next p loop to next p loop on 1st medallion and following 3 p loops to next 3 p loops on neckband, finish rnd with no more joinings. Fasten off.

Make 7 more medallions, joining them as 2nd medallion was joined to 1st. Fasten off.

With right side facing attach thread in 2nd free p loop on 1st medallion, ch 7 (to count as tr tr), d tr in next p loop, * (make a p loop, in next p loop make sc, p loop and sc) 3 times; make a p loop, d tr in next p loop, tr tr in joining of next p loops, d tr in next p loop of next medallion. Repeat from * across, ending with (make a p loop, in next p loop make sc, p loop and sc) 3 times; make a p loop, d tr in next p loop, tr tr in next p loop (63 p loops). Turn. 2nd row: Make a p loop, sc in tr tr, (make a p loop, in next p loop make sc, p loop and sc) 4 times; (p loop, sc in next p loop) 3 times; make a p loop, in tr tr make sc, p loop and sc, (p loop, sc in next p loop) 3 times; (p loop, in next p loop make sc, p loop and sc) 4 times; make a p loop, in tr tr make sc, p loop and sc, (p loop, in next p loop make sc, p loop and sc) 4 times; (p loop, sc in next p loop) 3 times; make a p loop, in tr tr make sc, p loop and sc, (p loop, sc in next p loop) 7 times; make a p loop, in tr tr make sc, p loop and sc, (p loop, in next p loop make sc, p loop and sc) 7 times; make a p loop, in tr tr make sc, p loop and sc, (p loop, sc in next p loop) 7 times; make a p loop, in tr tr make sc, p loop and sc, (p loop, sc in next p loop) 3 times; (p loop, in next p loop make sc, p loop and sc) 4 times; make a p loop, in tr tr make sc, p loop and sc, (p loop,

in next p loop make sc, p loop and sc) 4 times; (p loop, sc in next p loop) 3 times; make a p loop, in tr tr make sc, p loop and sc, (p loop, sc in next loop) 3 times; (p loop, in next p loop make sc, p loop and sc) 4 times; make a p loop, sc in top st of turning ch (112 p loops). Turn. 3rd row: Sl st to center of 1st p loop, ch 1, sc in same place, * make a p loop, sc in next p loop. Repeat from * across ending with p loop, join with sl st in 1st sc made (112 p loops).

Hereafter work is done in rnds. Next rnd: Sl st to center of 1st p loop, ch 1, sc in same place, * make a p loop, sc in next p loop. Repeat from * around. Join last p loop with sl st in 1st sc made (112 p loops). Turn. Repeat last rnd until piece measures 4½ inches (5 inches) from neck edge. Turn. Next rnd: Sl st to center of 1st p loop, ch 1, sc in same place, (make a p loop, sc in next p loop) 18 times; make a p loop, sk next 20 p loops (sleeve) sc in next p loop, (make a p loop, sc in next p loop) 35 times; make a p loop, sk next 20 p loops (sleeve), sc in next p loop, (make a p loop, sc in next p loop) 16 times; make a p loop, sl st in 1st sc made (72 p loops). Turn. Continue working over these 72 p loops as before until piece measures 12½ inches (13½ inches) from center front neck edge or length desired. Join and fasten off.

First Medallion . . . Work as for 1st medallion of neck edge until 6th rnd is completed. 7th rnd: Sl st to center of 1st p loop, ch 6, sc in 4th ch from hook, ch 1, sc in any p loop on last rnd of dress, ch 5, sc in 4th ch from hook, ch 3, sc in next p loop on medallion, * ch 6, sc in 4th ch from hook, ch 1, sc in next p loop on dress, ch 5, sc in 4th ch

from hook, ch 3, sc in next p loop on medallion. Repeat from * two more times (4 joinings). Complete medallion. Fasten off.

Second Medallion . . . Work as for 1st medallion until 6th rnd is completed. 7th rnd: Sl st to center of 1st p loop, ch 6, sc in 4th ch from hook, ch 1, sc in 2nd p loop (from last joining) on 1st medallion, join next p loop to next p loop on 1st medallion and the following 4 p loops to next 4 p loops on dress, finish medallion with no more joinings. Fasten off.

Make 16 more medallions, joining them as 2nd medallion was joined to 1st and joining last medallion to 1st medallion. Fasten off.

SLEEVES . . . Attach thread in next free p loop of Sleeve, ch 1, sc in same place where thread was attached, * make a p loop, sk next p loop, sc in next p loop, (make a p loop, sc in next p loop) 3 times. Repeat from * around to last p loop, ch 6, sc in 4th ch from hook, tr tr in joining of next p loops on skirt, ch 5, sc in 4th ch from hook, ch 3, join with sl st in 1st sc made (16 p loops).

Now work 4 medallions and attach to last 16 p loops same as medallions were attached to lower edge of skirt. Fasten off. Attach thread at right back neck edge. * Ch 5, sc in next p loop. Repeat from * to base of back opening. Ch 2, sc in next p loop on opposite edge. Work ch-5 loops up left side to neck edge. Ch 1, turn. Now work 7 sc in each ch-5 loop around. Fasten off. Sew button to left back neck edge and use a loop on right edge for buttonhole.

Press lightly on wrong side through damp cloth on a well-padded surface.

ROSE OF TRALEE

(Continued from page 41)

petal of rose, ° ch 1, cluster st in same space on center, ch 4, s c in the ch 1 between next 2 cluster sts, ch 4, cluster st in next ch 5 loop, ch 1, s c in center st of next petal of same rose, ch 1, cluster st in same space on center, ch 4, s c in next ch 1 loop between next 2 cluster sts, ch 4, cluster st in next ch 5 loop, ch 1, join to center st of any petal of next rose, repeat from ° until all roses are joined ending to correspond, join, cut thread.

LEAF: With Green ch 11, s c in 2nd st from hook, 1 s c in each of the next 8 sts of ch, 3 s c in last st, working on other side of ch, 1 s c in each of the next 8 sts.

2nd Row. Ch 2, turn, working through back loop of sts only, skip 1 s c, 1 s c in each of the next 8 s c, 3 s c in next s c, 1 s c in each of the next 8 s c.
Repeat the 2nd row 5 times.

Next Round. Ch 1, turn, join to center st of 2nd free petal on right hand side of any rose (to join: drop loop from hook, insert in petal, pick up loop and pull through), skip 1 s c on leaf and working through back loop of sts only, 1 s c in each of the next 9 s c, join to center st of next free petal of same rose, s c in same space on leaf, join to center st of 1st free petal on left hand side of next rose, s c in same space on leaf, 1 s c in each of the next 8 s c, join to center st of next petal of same rose, ch 1, s c in next s c on leaf, cut thread. Work 9 more leaves joining between roses in same manner.

IRISH CROCHET . . . TO CHERISH FOREVER

(Continued from page 10)

picot loop, s c between picots of next loop, repeat from * all around.

8th Row. Ch 10, * sl st in 5th st from hook for picot, ch 7, sl st in 5th st from hook for picot, ch 2, s c between picots of next loop, ch 7, s c between picots of next loop, ch 7, sl st in 5th st from hook for picot, ch 7, sl st in 5th st from hook for picot, d c in next s c of last row, ch 7, repeat from * all around and sl st in 3rd st of ch 10.

9th Row. Sl st between next 2 picots, * work a double picot loop, 7 d c over ch 7 of last row, double picot loop, s c between picots of next loop, ch 7, s c between picots of next loop, repeat from * all around.

10th Row. Sl st between picots, * double picot loop, s c in 4th d c, ch 5, s c in same st, double picot loop, s c between picots of next loop, double picot loop, 7 d c over ch 7, double picot loop, s c between picots of next loop and repeat from * all around.

11th Row. Sl st between picots, * double picot loop, s c between picots of next loop, double picot loop, s c between picots of next loop, double picot loop, s c in 4th d c, ch 5, s c in same space, double picot loop, s c between next 2 picots, double picot loop, s c between picots of next loop, and repeat from * all around.

PLACEMATS WITH ROSE BORDER

(Continued from page 11)

Work another flower same as previous flowers but leaving 4 petals free on outside edge of previous flower for corner when joining. Work 8 more flowers joining same as 1st side. Work another flower and join to last flower leaving 4 petals free on outside edge of last flower made for corner. Work 13 flowers joining same as 1st side. Work another flower and join to last flower leaving 4 petals free on outside edge of last flower for corner. Work 7 more flowers joining same as 1st side and joining last flower to 1st flower made leaving 4 petals free on outside edge of 1st flower for corner.
Cut linen ½ inch larger all around than inside edge, turn under a narrow hem and sew. Attach Nile Green at corner of linen, 3 s c in same space, ** 1 d c between the 2 petals of corner flower, 2 s c in same space on linen, working the s c about 1/16 inch apart work 2 s c on linen, 1 tr c in joining of corner flower and next flower to left of corner, 6 s c on linen, drop loop from hook, insert in center of 1st free petal of 1st flower to left of corner, pick up loop and pull through, 5 s c on linen, join to center of next petal of same flower, * 6 s c on linen, 1 tr c in joining of flowers, 6 s c on linen, join to center of 1st free petal of next flower, 5 s c on linen, join to next free petal of same flower, repeat from * to corner, 6 s c on linen, 1 tr c in joining of last flower and next corner flower, 2 s c on linen, 3 s c in corner of linen, repeat from ** all around, cut thread. Work other 3 mats in same manner.

NAPKINS: Cut linen 12 x 12 inches. Turn under a very narrow hem and sew. With Nile Green work a row of s c around entire napkin working 5 s c in each corner, join, cut thread. Attach Shaded Pinks at corner, ch 3, d c in same space, ch 3, sl st in top of last d c for picot, d c in same space, * ch 3, skip 2 s c, s c in next s c, ch 3, skip 2 s c, 2 d c in next s c, ch 3, sl st in top of last d c for picot, d c in same space, repeat from * all around working the 2 d c, picot, 1 d c at each corner and ending row to correspond, join, cut thread. Work a rose same as on mat and applique to corner as illustrated.

COBWEBBY BORDERS

(Continued from page 13)

in the rnd—*to inc, make 2 tr in 1 st.* Join (60 tr). **5th rnd:** Sc in same place as sl st, * ch 2, skip 2 sts, tr in next st, ch 2; d tr in each of next 5 sts with ch-2 between; ch 2, tr in next st, ch 2, skip 2 sts, sc in next st. Repeat from * around (5 fans). **6th rnd:** * 2 sc in next sp; in each of next 6 sps make 2 sc, ch 3, 2 sc; 2 sc in next sp. Repeat from * around; sl st in 1st sc made. Fasten off. Sew a Center Flower to center of Motif. This completes Motif. Make an even number of Motifs. Now make an uneven number of Center Flowers.

Joining Flowers and Motifs . . .
Attach thread to 4th st to the right of the base of any petal on a Flower. * Ch 6, sc in 3rd ch from hook (p made), ch 3, p, ch 3 (a p loop made), sc in 4th st from beginning of next petal, p loop, sc in 4th st from end of same petal. Repeat from * once more, make a p loop, sc in 4th st from beginning of next petal. Ch 4, sc in 2nd p to the right of base of any scallop on a Motif. Fasten off. * * Skip 2 complete scallops on Motif, attach thread in 2nd p on next scallop, ch 4, sc in 4th st to the right of the base of any petal on another Flower (make a p loop, sc in 4th st from beginning of next petal, p loop, sc in 4th st from end of same petal) twice; make a p loop, sc in 4th st from beginning of next petal, ch 4, sc in 2nd p to the right of base of any scallop on another Motif. Fasten off. Repeat from * * until piece is length desired, ending with a Flower.

Heading . . . 1st row: Attach thread in 2nd p loop on 1st Flower, ch 5, (p, ch 3) twice; * sc in next p loop, make a p loop, dc in next p loop, (ch 3, p) twice; ch 2, holding back the last loop of each st on hook make d tr in next p loop, dc in 2nd p on 1st free scallop on next motif, thread over and draw through all loops on hook, make a p loop, skip next p on Motif, sc in next p, make a p loop, skip next p, holding back the last loop of each dc on hook make dc in each of next 2 p's, thread over and draw through all loops on hook, make a p loop, skip next p, sc in next p, make a p loop, skip next p, holding back the last loop of each st on hook make dc in next p, d tr in next p loop on next Flower, make a p loop, dc in next p loop, make a p loop. Repeat from * across, ending with dc in last p loop. Make a p loop, turn. **2nd and 3rd rows:** Sc in next p loop, * make a p loop, sc in next p loop. Repeat from * across. Make a p loop, turn. At end of 3rd row ch 10, turn. **4th row:** 2 dc in next p loop, * ch 6, 2 dc in next p loop. Repeat from * across. Ch 3, turn. **5th row:** Dc in next dc, * ch 6, dc in each of next 2 dc. Repeat from * across, ending with ch 4, skip 4 ch, dc in next ch. Fasten off.

EDGINGS FOR THAT SPECIAL GIFT
(Continued from page 15)

EDGINGS FOR THAT SPECIAL GIFT

length desired, having a multiple of 5 plus 4 tr groups. Ch 3, turn and work scallops along long edge as follows: **1st row:** * (In the tip of next cluster make tr, ch 4 and tr) 4 times; ch 4, sk tip of next cluster. Repeat from * across. Ch 4, turn. **2nd row:** * (Tr in next tr, ch 4, tr in next tr) 3 times; (ch 4, sc in next tr) twice; ch 4. Repeat from * across, ending with ch 4, sc in last tr. Ch 7, turn. **3rd row:** * In next tr make tr, ch 4 and tr, tr in next tr, ch 4, make a 3-tr cluster in each of the next 2 tr, ch 4, tr in next tr, in next tr make tr, ch 4 and tr, ch 4. Repeat from * across. Ch 4, turn. **4th row:** * Tr in next tr, ch 4, tr in next tr, in tip of next cluster make a 3-tr cluster, ch 4 and a 3-tr cluster, tr in next tr, ch 4, tr in next tr, (ch 4, sc in next tr) twice; ch 4. Repeat from * across, ending with tr in last tr. Turn. **5th row:** Sl st in next tr, * ch 4, tr in next tr, in next loop make (tr, ch 3, sc in 3rd ch from hook) 4 times and tr; tr in next tr, ch 4, sc in next tr, (ch 4, sc in next sc) twice; ch 4, sc in next tr. Repeat from * across. Fasten off.

No. 3-38 . . . Make a loose chain slightly longer than length desired. **1st row:** Dc in 6th ch from hook, * ch 1, sk 1 ch, dc in next ch. Repeat from * across for length desired (number of sps must be a multiple of 4 plus 1). Turn. Cut off remaining chain. **2nd row:** Sl st into sp, ch 7, dc in same sp, * sk 1 sp, in next sp work dc, ch 5 and dc. Repeat from * across, turn. **3rd row:** Sl st into ch-5 loop, ch 7, dc in same loop, * in next loop work dc, ch 5 and dc. Repeat from * across. Turn. **4th row:** * 2 sc in next loop, (ch 5, 2 sc in same loop) 3 times; 5 sc in next loop. Repeat from * across. Fasten off.

KILLARNEY BEDSPREAD

(Continued from page 19)

of next Square) 8 times. Repeat from * to *. * * (Ch 8, p, ch 12, p, ch 4, 1 sc in corner of next Square) 6 times, ch 8, p, ch 4, sk next Corner Square, 1 sc across in corner of next Square, (ch 8, p, ch 12, p, ch 4, 1 sc in corner of next Square) 6 times. Repeat from * to *. Repeat from * * around Spread, making each Corner Block the same as first one. Fasten off. **3rd ROW:** Join to center of 1st p-loop of last row, (ch 8, p, ch 12, p, ch 4, 1 sc in next p-loop) 5 times, (ch 8, p, ch 12, p, ch 4, 1 dc in next d tr) twice, (ch 8, p, ch 12, p, ch 4, 1 sc in next 2-p-loop) 8 times, (ch 8, p, ch 12, p, ch 4, 1 dc in next d tr) twice, (ch 8, p, ch 12, p, ch 4, 1 sc in next loop) 6 times, ch 8, p, ch 4, 1 sc across corner in next 2-p-loop. Continue on around in same way and fasten off. **4th ROW:** Join to 1st p-loop of last row, (ch 8, p, ch 12, p, ch 4, 1 sc in next loop) 6 times, ch 8, p, ch 12, p, ch 4, 1 sc in same corner loop, (ch 8, p, ch 12, p, ch 4, 1 sc in next loop) 10 times, ch 8, p, ch 12, p, ch 4, 1 sc in same corner loop, (ch 8, p, ch 12, p, ch 4, 1 sc in next loop) 6 times, ch 8, p, ch 4, 1 sc across corner in next 2-p-loop. Continue on around and fasten off. **5th ROW:** Join to center st between ps of 1st loop of last row, * ch 7, a 3d tr-Cluster in same st, a 5-ch p in top of Cluster, (ch 5, 1 sc in 1st st for a p) 4 times, ch 3, 1 sl st in center st of next p-loop. * Repeat from * to * 22 times around Corner Block. * * (Ch 5, 1 sc in 1st st for a p) 4 times, ch 1, 1 sc across corner in next 2-p-loop. Repeat from * to * 12 times. Repeat from * * around, making each Corner Block the same as first one. Fasten off, and steam and press Edge in sections, stretching out and pinning down each point.

ROSE WREATH

(Continued from page 25)

LEAF (Make 10) . . . Starting at center, ch 10. **1st row:** Sc in 2nd ch from hook, sc in each ch across, 3 sc in last ch; working along opposite side of starting chain, make sc in next 7 ch. Ch 1, turn. **2nd to 10th rows incl:** Picking up back loop only, sc in each sc to within center sc of next 3-sc group, 3 sc in next sc, sc in each remaining sc to within last sc. Ch 1, turn. At end of 10th row, ch 5, turn. **11th and 12th rows:** Sc in 2nd ch from hook, sc in next 3 ch, picking up back loop only, sc in each sc to within center sc of next 3-sc group, 3 sc in next sc, sc in each remaining sc to within last sc. Ch 5, turn. At end of 12th row, ch 1, turn. **13th to 17th rows incl:** Repeat 2nd row. At end of 17th row, ch 5, turn. **18th and 19th rows:** Repeat 11th and 12th rows once more. **20th to 27th rows incl:** Repeat 2nd row. Break off at end of 27th row.

FLOWER (Make 10) . . . Starting at center, ch 20. Join with sl st to form ring. **1st rnd:** Cut 16 strands of thread, each 10 inches long. Working over these strands, make 40 sc in ring. Join to first sc. Cut off remaining strands. **2nd rnd:** Ch 1, sc in each sc around. Join. Now work petal in rows as follows: Ch 17. **1st row:** Dc in 4th ch from hook, dc in next 7 ch, half dc in next ch, sc in next 5 ch. Sl st in next sc on last rnd. Carry thread behind work and draw loop on hook across to next free sc on last rnd, sl st in same place, sc in first ch on opposite side of starting chain of petal, sc in next 4 ch, half dc in next ch, dc in next 8 ch, 2 dc in next ch, dc in next ch, 2 dc in next dc, dc in next 8 dc, half dc in next half dc, sc in next 5 sc. Sl st in next sc on last rnd. Ch 1, turn. **2nd row:** Sc in next 5 sc on Petal, half dc in next half dc, dc in next 8 dc, (2 dc in next dc, dc in next dc) 3 times; dc in next 7 dc, half dc in next half dc, sc in next 5 sc. Sl st in next sc on last rnd. Break off. Skip 5 sc on last rnd, attach thread to next sc, ch 17 and complete another Petal. Make 3 more Petals the same way.

Sew Flowers and Leaves in place around Doily. Starch lightly and press.

EMERALD ISLE TABLECLOTH

(Continued from page 22)

sc, ch 3 and sc; (ch 6, in next ch-6 loop make sc, ch 3 and sc) 3 times; * ch 6, in sp between clusters make cluster, ch 5 and cluster; (ch 6, in next ch-6 loop make sc, ch 3 and sc) 6 times. Repeat from * around, ending with ch 6, sl st in first sc made. Join and break off.

SECOND MOTIF . . . Work as for First Motif until 7 rnds are completed. **8th rnd:** In sp make sc, ch 3 and sc, (ch 6, in next loop make sc, ch 3 and sc) 3 times; ch 6, in sp between clusters make cluster, ch 5 and cluster, (ch 3, sl st in corresponding loop on First Motif. ch 3, in next loop on Second Motif make sc, ch 3 and sc) 6 times; ch 3, sl st in corresponding loop on First Motif, ch 3, in sp between clusters on Second Motif make cluster, ch 5 and cluster. Complete rnd as for First Motif (no more joinings).

Make 22 rows of 28 motifs, joining adjacent sides as Second Motif was joined to First Motif.

EDGING . . . 1st rnd: Attach thread to any corner loop, sc in same loop, * (ch 10, sc in next loop) 7 times; (ch 10, sc in next ch-5 loop) twice. Repeat from * around, ending with ch 10, sl st in first sc. **2nd rnd:** 13 sc in each loop around. Join and break off. Starch lightly and press.

IRISH MIST CENTERPIECE

(Continued from page 23)

ch 1, turn, 4 s c, picot, 4 s c over each 6 ch loop, sl st in next d c, 5 d c, picot, 10 d c over remainder of ch 15, ch 3, sl st in same loop, 5 d c over remainder of next loop, ch 3, sl st in same loop, 5 d c over remainder of next loop, ch 3, sl st in same loop, 3 s c over remainder of ch 11 of previous row and repeat from ** 4 times, fasten thread.

Join thread in corner of 2nd right hand scallop, ch 7, picot, ch 3, d tr c in center s c between scallops, ch 7, picot, ch 3, sl st in corner of 2nd scallop, ch 5, turn, picot, ch 5, picot, ch 1, d tr c in d tr c, ch 5, picot, ch 7, picot, ch 1, d tr c in same space, ch 5, picot, ch 5, picot, ch 2, sl st in 2nd d c of center scallop, fasten thread.

Join thread on wrong side of work in 5th d c of next scallop, ch 6, d tr c in next d tr c, ch 6, d tr c between next 2 picots, ch 6, d tr c in same space, ch 6, d tr c in next d tr c, ch 6, join in 5th d c of scallop, ch 1, turn, 4 s c, picot, 4 s c over each loop, fasten thread.

Join motifs at 7 picots on each side.

There are 5 motifs in the center row, 4 on each side of center and 3 motifs at each end.

BOUQUET

(Continued from page 24)

ch-5 loop on Center, ch 3, sc in same dc on Second Flower. Complete rnd as before, no more joinings.

Make 18 more flowers, joining adjacent sides as Second Flower was joined to First Flower and Center. Join Last and First Flowers together as before.

SECOND RND OF FLOWERS—First Flower . . . Starting at center with Blue, ch 10. Join with sl st to form ring. Work as for Center until 7 rnds are completed. **8th rnd:** In each sp around make sc, 5 dc and sc. Join and break off. **9th rnd:** Attach Green to first sc on any scallop, sc in same place, ch 3, skip 2 dc, in next dc, ch 3, sl st in center loop of any flower on previous rnd, ch 3, sc in same dc on flower in work, * ch 3, sc in first sc on next scallop, ch 3, skip 2 dc, in next dc make sc, ch 3 and sc. Repeat from * around. Join and break off.

SECOND FLOWER . . . Work as for First Flower until 8 rnds are completed. **9th rnd:** Attach Green to first sc of any scallop, sc in same place, ch 2, skip 2 dc, sc in next dc, ch 2, sl st in 2nd loop following joining on First Flower, ch 2, sc in same dc on Second Flower, ch 2, sc in first sc on next scallop, ch 2, skip 2 dc, in next dc make sc, ch 3 and sc; ch 2, sc in first sc on next scallop, ch 2, skip 2 dc, sc in next dc, ch 3, sl st in center loop on next flower on previous rnd, ch 3, sc in same dc on Second Flower, complete rnd, no more joinings. Make 18 more flowers, joining adjacent sides as Second Flower was joined to First Flower and previous rnd.

THIRD RND OF FLOWERS — First Flower . . . Starting at center with Blue, ch 10. Work as for Center until 9 rnds are completed. **10th rnd:** In each sp around make sc, 7 dc and sc. Join and break off. **11th rnd:** Attach Green to first sc of any scallop, sc in same place, ch 4, skip 3 dc, sc in next dc, ch 3, sl st in center loop on any flower on previous rnd, ch 3, sc in same dc on flower in work, (ch 4, sc in first sc on next scallop, ch 4, skip 3 dc, in next dc make sc, ch 3 and sc) 4 times; ch 4, sc in first sc on next scallop, ch 4, skip 3 dc, in next dc make sc, ch 6 and sc. Complete rnd making ch 3 loops on each remaining scallop. Join and break off.

SECOND FLOWER . . . Work as for First Flower until 10 rnds are completed. **11th rnd:** Attach Green to first sc on any scallop, sc in same place, ch 4, skip 3 dc, sc in next dc, ch 4, sc in 2nd loop following joining on First Flower, ch 4, sc in same dc on Second Flower, ch 4, sc in first sc on next scallop, ch 4, skip 3 dc, in next dc make sc, ch 3 and sc; ch 4, sc in first sc on next scallop, ch 3, sl st in center loop on next flower on previous rnd, ch 3, sc in same dc on Second Flower, (ch 4, sc in first sc on next scallop, ch 4, skip 3 dc, in next dc make sc, ch 3 and sc) 4 times; ch 4, sc in first sc on next scallop, ch 4, skip 3 dc, in next dc make sc, ch 6 and sc. Complete rnd as before, no more joinings. Join and break off.

LAST RND OF MOTIFS—First Motif . . . Starting at center with Lt. Steel Blue, ch 9. Join with sl st to form ring. Work as for Center until 3 rnds are completed. **4th rnd:** In each sp around make sc, 3 dc and sc. Join and break off. **5th rnd:** Attach Green to first sc on any scallop, sc in same place, * ch 1, skip 1 dc, in next dc make sc, ch 3 and sc; ch 1, sc in first sc of next scallop. Repeat from * around. Join and break off.

LEAF . . . Starting at center with White Tatting Cotton and No. 14 hook, ch 13. **1st row:** Sc in 2nd ch from hook and each ch across, 3 sc in last ch. Working along opposite side of starting chain make sc in each ch across. Ch 1, turn. **2nd row:** Sc in each sc across, making 3 sc in center sc of 3-sc group. Ch 1, turn. **3rd to 6th rows incl:** Sc in each sc across to within last sc, making 3 sc in center sc of 3-sc group. Ch 1, turn. **7th row:** Sc in each sc across to center sc of 3-sc group, 2 sc in center sc, sl st in any loop on motif, sc in same sc on leaf, sc in each remaining sc to within last sc. Break off. Make 8 more leaves, joining them to motif as before. Sew leaves together, joining 10 sc on last row of each side of leaf.

Make 19 more motifs in this manner. Sew motifs together, joining ends of 2 leaves, and having 3 leaves free on inner side of motif and 4 leaves free on outer edge. Sew motifs around doily, joining center free leaf to ch-6 loop on motif of previous rnd. Starch lightly and press.

Simple Crochet Stitches

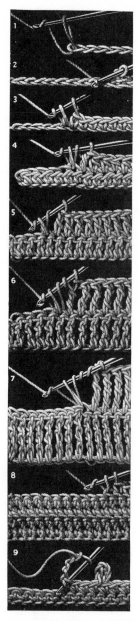

No. 1—Chain Stitch (CH) Form a loop on thread insert hook on loop and pull thread through tightening threads. Thread over hook and pull through last chain made. Continue chains for length desired.

No. 2—Slip Stitch (SL ST) Make a chain the desired length. Skip one chain, * insert hook in next chain, thread over hook and pull through stitch and loop on hook. Repeat from *. This stitch is used in joining and whenever an invisible stitch is required.

No. 3—Single Crochet (S C) Chain for desired length, skip 1 ch, * insert hook in next ch, thread over hook and pull through ch. There are now 2 loops on hook, thread over hook and pull through both loops, repeat from *. For succeeding rows of s c, ch 1, turn insert hook in top of next st taking up both threads and continue same as first row.

No. 4—Short Double Crochet (S D C) Ch for desired length thread over hook, insert hook in 3rd st from hook, draw thread through (3 loops on hook), thread over and draw through all three loops on hook. For succeeding rows, ch 2, turn.

No. 5—Double Crochet (D C) Ch for desired length, thread over hook, insert hook in 4th st from hook, draw thread through (3 loops on hook) thread over hook and pull through 2 loops thread over hook and pull through 2 loops. Succeeding rows, ch 3, turn and work next d c in 2nd d c of previous row. The ch 3 counts as 1 d c.

No. 6—Treble Crochet (TR C) Ch for desired length, thread over hook twice insert hook in 5th ch from hook draw thread through (4 loops on hook) thread over hook pull through 2 loops thread over, pull through 2 loops, thread over, pull through 2 loops. For succeeding rows ch 4, turn and work next tr c in 2nd tr c of previous row. The ch 4 counts as 1 tr c.

No. 7—Double Treble Crochet (D TR C) Ch for desired length thread over hook 3 times insert in 6th ch from hook (5 loops on hook) and work off 2 loops at a time same as tr c. For succeeding rows ch 5 turn and work next d tr c in 2nd d tr c of previous row. The ch 5 counts as 1 d tr c.

No. 8—Rib Stitch. Work this same as single crochet but insert hook in back loop of stitch only. This is sometimes called the slipper stitch.

No. 9—Picot (P) There are two methods of working the picot. (A) Work a single crochet in the foundation, ch 3 or 4 sts depending on the length of picot desired, sl st in top of s c made. (B) Work an s c, ch 3 or 4 for picot and s c in same space. Work as many single crochets between picots as desired.

No. 10—Open or Filet Mesh (O M.) When worked on a chain work the first d c in 8th ch from hook * ch 2, skip 2 sts, 1 d c in next st, repeat from *. Succeeding rows ch 5 to turn, d c in d c, ch 2, d c in next d c, repeat from *.

No. 11—Block or Solid Mesh (S M) Four double crochets form 1 solid mesh and 3 d c are required for each additional solid mesh. Open mesh and solid mesh are used in Filet Crochet.

No. 12—Slanting Shell St. Ch for desired length, work 2 d c in 4th st from hook, skip 3 sts, sl st in next st, * ch 3, 2 d c in same st with sl st, skip 3 sts, sl st in next st. Repeat from *. **2nd Row.** Ch 3, turn 2 d c in sl st, sl st in 3 ch loop of shell in previous row, * ch 3, 2 d c in same space, sl st in next shell, repeat from *.

No. 13—Bean or Pop Corn Stitch. Work 3 d c in same space, drop loop from hook insert hook in first d c made and draw loop through, ch 1 to tighten st.

No. 14—Cross Treble Crochet. Ch for desired length, thread over twice, insert in 5th st from hook, * work off two loops, thread over, skip 2 sts, insert in next st and work off all loops on needle 2 at a time, ch 2, d c in center to complete cross. Thread over twice, insert in next st and repeat from *.

No. 15—Cluster Stitch. Work 3 or 4 tr c in same st always retaining the last loop of each tr c on needle, thread over and pull through all loops on needle.

No. 16—Lacet St. Ch for desired length, work 1 s c in 10th st from hook, ch 3 skip 2 sts, 1 d c in next st, * ch 3, skip 2 sts, 1 s c in next st, ch 3, skip 2 sts 1 d c in next st, repeat from * to end of row, 2nd row, d c in d c, ch 5 d c in next d c.

No. 17—Knot Stitch (Sometimes Called Lovers Knot St.) Ch for desired length, * draw a ¼ inch loop on hook, thread over and pull through ch, s c in single loop of st, draw another ¼ inch loop, s c into loop, skip 4 sts, s c in next st, repeat from *. To turn make ⅜" knots, * s c in loop at right of s c and s c in loop at left of s c of previous row, 2 knot sts and repeat from *.

Metric Conversion Chart

CONVERTING INCHES TO CENTIMETERS AND YARDS TO METERS

mm — millimeters   cm — centimeters   m — meters

INCHES INTO MILLIMETERS AND CENTIMETERS
(Slightly rounded off for convenience)

inches	mm		cm	inches	cm	inches	cm	inches	cm
⅛	3mm			5	12.5	21	53.5	38	96.5
¼	6mm			5½	14	22	56	39	99
⅜	10mm	or	1cm	6	15	23	58.5	40	101.5
½	13mm	or	1.3cm	7	18	24	61	41	104
⅝	15mm	or	1.5cm	8	20.5	25	63.5	42	106.5
¾	20mm	or	2cm	9	23	26	66	43	109
⅞	22mm	or	2.2cm	10	25.5	27	68.5	44	112
1	25mm	or	2.5cm	11	28	28	71	45	114.5
1¼	32mm	or	3.2cm	12	30.5	29	73.5	46	117
1½	38mm	or	3.8cm	13	33	30	76	47	119.5
1¾	45mm	or	4.5cm	14	35.5	31	79	48	122
2	50mm	or	5cm	15	38	32	81.5	49	124.5
2½	65mm	or	6.5cm	16	40.5	33	84	50	127
3	75mm	or	7.5cm	17	43	34	86.5		
3½	90mm	or	9cm	18	46	35	89		
4	100mm	or	10cm	19	48.5	36	91.5		
4½	115mm	or	11.5cm	20	51	37	94		

YARDS TO METERS
(Slightly rounded off for convenience)

yards	meters	yards	meters	yards	meters	yards	meters	yards	meters
⅛	0.15	2⅛	1.95	4⅛	3.80	6⅛	5.60	8⅛	7.45
¼	0.25	2¼	2.10	4¼	3.90	6¼	5.75	8¼	7.55
⅜	0.35	2⅜	2.20	4⅜	4.00	6⅜	5.85	8⅜	7.70
½	0.50	2½	2.30	4½	4.15	6½	5.95	8½	7.80
⅝	0.60	2⅝	2.40	4⅝	4.25	6⅝	6.10	8⅝	7.90
¾	0.70	2¾	2.55	4¾	4.35	6¾	6.20	8¾	8.00
⅞	0.80	2⅞	2.65	4⅞	4.50	6⅞	6.30	8⅞	8.15
1	0.95	3	2.75	5	4.60	7	6.40	9	8.25
1⅛	1.05	3⅛	2.90	5⅛	4.70	7⅛	6.55	9⅛	8.35
1¼	1.15	3¼	3.00	5¼	4.80	7¼	6.65	9¼	8.50
1⅜	1.30	3⅜	3.10	5⅜	4.95	7⅜	6.75	9⅜	8.60
1½	1.40	3½	3.20	5½	5.05	7½	6.90	9½	8.70
1⅝	1.50	3⅝	3.35	5⅝	5.15	7⅝	7.00	9⅝	8.80
1¾	1.60	3¾	3.45	5¾	5.30	7¾	7.10	9¾	8.95
1⅞	1.75	3⅞	3.55	5⅞	5.40	7⅞	7.20	9⅞	9.05
2	1.85	4	3.70	6	5.50	8	7.35	10	9.15

AVAILABLE FABRIC WIDTHS

25″	65cm	50″	127cm
27″	70cm	54″/56″	140cm
35″/36″	90cm	58″/60″	150cm
39″	100cm	68″/70″	175cm
44″/45″	115cm	72″	180cm
48″	122cm		

AVAILABLE ZIPPER LENGTHS

4″	10cm	10″	25cm	22″	55cm
5″	12cm	12″	30cm	24″	60cm
6″	15cm	14″	35cm	26″	65cm
7″	18cm	16″	40cm	28″	70cm
8″	20cm	18″	45cm	30″	75cm
9″	22cm	20″	50cm		